D0166360

PARAGRAPH
DEVELOPMENT

A Guide for
Students of English

SECOND EDITION

MARTIN L. ARNAUDET
MARY ELLEN BARRETT

English Language Institute
The American University
Washington, D. C.

PRENTICE HALL REGENTS
Englewood Cliffs, New Jersey 07632

Library of Congress Cataloging-in-Publication Data

Arnaudet, Martin L.
    Paragraph development : a guide for students of English / Martin
L. Arnaudet, Mary Ellen Barrett.—2nd ed.
    p.
    ISBN 0-13-648502-2
    1. English language—Textbooks for foreign speakers. 2. English
language—Paragraphs. I. Barrett, Mary Ellen. II. Title.
PE1128.A67 1990   89-28036
808'.042—dc20   CIP

Editorial/production supervision and
    interior design: Noël Vreeland Carter
Cover design: 20/20 Services, Inc.
Manufacturing buyer: Ray Keating
Illustration on Page 84 by Alexandra Schultz

©1990 by Prentice Hall Regents
Prentice-Hall, Inc.
A Paramount Communications Company
Englewood Cliffs, New Jersey 07632

For Gordon

All rights reserved. No part of this book may be
reproduced, in any form or by any means,
without permission in writing from the publisher.

Printed in the United States of America
10 9 8 7 6

ISBN 0-13-648502-2

Prentice-Hall International (UK) Limited, *London*
Prentice-Hall of Australia Pty. Limited, *Sydney*
Prentice-Hall Canada Inc., *Toronto*
Prentice-Hall Hispanoamericana, S.A., *Mexico*
Prentice-Hall of India Private Limited, *New Delhi*
Prentice-Hall of Japan, Inc., *Tokyo*
Simon & Schuster Asia Pte. Ltd., *Singapore*
Editora Prentice-Hall do Brasil, Ltda., *Rio de Janeiro*

CONTENTS

PREFACE

Paragraph Development is an integrated guide for high intermediate to advanced learners of English. It focuses on the physical paragraph as a basic unit of composition common to most forms of academic, business, professional, and general-purpose writing. It is designed to be flexible enough to be used as a writing component in an intensive or semi-intensive program or as an independent writing course. The book is based on the theory that if a student is able to write a unified, coherent paragraph, transferring this skill to full composition writing will not be difficult. The approach in each chapter is direct and functional: a model is provided and graphically explained; then the student is asked to imitate the model.

In the second edition, which maintains the same basic approach as the first, certain models have been updated, and the methodology has been slightly modified to reflect current pedagogical thought. The new features include:

Controlled Information Transfer exercises, which focus on interpretation of graphically represented data and provide another model of the type of paragraph being presented;

A choice of writing topics in each unit geared towards **general or academic subjects** (these posed as essay questions);

Three-phase writing assignments which emphasize writing as an **on-going process of planning, writing, and revising;**

Addition of **structures of definition** (adjective modifiers) in the paraphrasing section of Unit 7 Definition; and

A **Teacher's Guide** with answers to exercises and suggestions for teaching the text.

Organization of the Material

Units One and Two deal with limiting and supporting topic sentences. In Unit One, students are directed from identifying elements which limit a topic to writing their own topic sentences. In Unit Two, they are asked to analyze, through diagrams, how supporting material (examples, details, anecdotes, and statistics) relates directly to the topic sentence and thus creates unity within the paragraph.

Units Three through Six deal with the rhetorical patterns most commonly found in expository writing (Enumeration, Process, Chronology, Cause and Effect, and Comparison and Contrast). Fictional narration has purposely been omitted as primarily a literary device. Each paragraph type is introduced with a model, followed by graphic analysis and controlled exercises which ultimately lead to a free writing assignment. Although this book is *not* intended as a grammar text, some structures are reviewed in these units as they apply to the specific type of paragraph being discussed.

Unit Seven treats Definition not as a rhetorical device in and of itself, but rather as a kind of writing which often employs a variety of rhetorical devices.

Unit Eight is concerned with transferring the patterns of paragraph development to full composition writing.

Special Features

1. Neither the model paragraphs nor the exercises have been simplified or edited for non-native speakers. Because the text is intended for use at a number of levels and in a variety of programs, items within exercises which are more difficult because of vocabulary, content, or length have been starred (*) to indicate to both teacher and student that they are more challenging.

2. In each unit, a "Now Ask Yourself" review exercise follows the presentation of any new material. These exercises force the student to integrate what he or she has previously learned, to reinterpret it, and to apply it to the task at hand. This spiraling of concepts ensures greater student involvement and conceptual mastery of the material.

3. The paraphrasing exercises in Units Three through Six provide the students with the opportunity to practice sentences typical of each pattern of development before incorporating these patterns into free writing assignments.

4. Charts and diagrams are used to illustrate relationships within paragraphs—and finally within longer pieces of discourse—and to provide a visual, structural focus. We have chosen to call them *paragraph analysis* exercises. They are, in point of fact, reading exercises of the "information transfer" type, proceeding from the verbal to the visual. These charts and diagrams can easily be adapted to an *academic outline format* at the discretion of the teacher.

5. "Information transfer" exercises proceeding in the other direction—i.e. from the visual to the verbal—take the student from an analytical/reading stage into controlled writing. We feel that this is a particularly important and useful skill for a student to acquire before attempting unstructured composition.

Acknowledgments

We are grateful to our colleagues at the English Language Institute for their comments and suggestions during the process of revision. In particular, we would like to thank Jack Ramsay, Barbara Chase, Laura Oberdorfer, Sherry Russell, Wayne Nass, and Joseph Roy, who gave generously of their time and experience in using the original version of the book. We would also like to thank Gilbert Couts, Director of the English Language Institute, for allowing us full access to word processing and copying equipment.

MLA
MEB
Washington, D.C.

1

THE TOPIC SENTENCE

Paragraph Unity

THE PARAGRAPH

In written form, English is divided into *paragraphs* to distinguish one main idea from other main ideas. The paragraph is the *basic unit of composition.*

Remember this:

1. *A paragraph is a group of sentences which develop one central idea.*

2. *The central idea is usually stated in a topic sentence.*

3. Every sentence in the paragraph must help the development of the topic sentence.

INDENTATION

The first sentence of a paragraph is always *indented* so that the reader will know that a new subject—or a different aspect of the same subject—is being dealt with. The writer does this by leaving a blank space at the beginning of the paragraph. Think of indentation as simply *another kind of punctuation*. Just as a sentence ends with a period (.), so each new paragraph begins with an *indentation*.

If you are not already familiar with the idea of indentation, be sure to study the following diagram very carefully:

PARAGRAPH INDENTATION

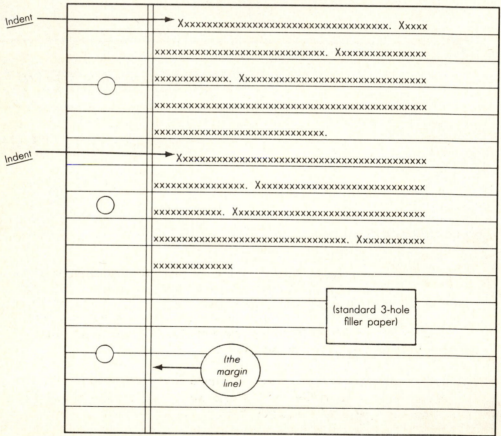

LENGTH

A paragraph may vary in length. Some paragraphs are quite short; others are extremely long. Most paragraphs have more than three sentences in them and usually have between 100 and 200 words.

Now Ask Yourself

1. What is a paragraph?_____

   _____

2. What is the proper "punctuation" for a paragraph?_____

   Where is it located in the paragraph?_____

3. How long should a paragraph be?_____

TOPIC VERSUS TOPIC SENTENCE

The first sentence of a paragraph is usually called the *topic sentence*. You may have noticed in your reading of certain English texts that it is possible to place the topic sentence at the *end* of the paragraph (as a kind of conclusion), or even in the *middle* (as a kind of link between the two parts). It is even possible not to have a topic sentence at all; in this case, we say that the topic sentence is *implied* or *suggested*. Be aware of these possibilities when you read; otherwise, you might miss the point which the author is trying to make. When you write, however, remember that a topic sentence placed at the beginning of a paragraph is the clearest kind of paragraph organization—simple, effective, easy for you to manage, and easy for your reader to understand.

What makes a good topic sentence? The most important thing to remember at this point is that in a topic sentence, always try to make a *statement* about your topic which *limits* it to a certain extent:

Topic Sentence = TOPIC + LIMITING STATEMENT

Take, for example, the general topic of *soccer*. There are too many things to say about soccer to put into a single paragraph. Therefore, your problem as a writer consists of deciding how you want to write about soccer. In other words, you need to *limit* your discussion.

One good way to limit your topic is to place *key words or phrases* in the topic sentence. These words or phrases will let the reader know how you are going to discuss the topic. These words or phrases are sometimes called *controlling words or phrases,* since they control the organization of the paragraph. In a paragraph on soccer, for example, they will immediately indicate to the reader that you plan to do *one* of several things:

Discuss the history of soccer

Compare it with another sport

Describe its difficulty

Explain the rules of the game

How do you limit a topic in a topic sentence? There are many ways, but the following is a list of the most common. Once you understand these examples, you will find it much easier to write a carefully controlled topic sentence.

Topic	Statement which Limits the Topic
1. Soccer	is now played <u>in the United States.</u> (place)
2. Soccer	has become more popular <u>within the last five years.</u> (time or period of time)
3. Soccer	is <u>a physically demanding sport.</u> (quality)
4. Soccer and football	<u>have a great deal in common.</u> (showing similarities)
5. Soccer	is <u>more dangerous than tennis.</u> (showing differences)
6. A soccer player	can receive <u>various kinds of penalties</u> (a number of things; a list) during a game.
7. The World Cup Soccer Champion-ship Games	<u>create interest</u> from soccer fans all over (effect) the world.
8. Soccer	is dangerous <u>for several reasons.</u> (cause; reason)

Now Ask Yourself ✎

1. Where does a topic sentence usually come in a paragraph?_____
2. Where else can it come?_____
3. What should a writer always try to do to the topic in a topic sentence?

_____

4. What are eight kinds of statements which a writer can use to limit his/ her topic?

   a. _____   e. _____

b. _____   f. _____

c. _____   g. _____

d. _____   h. _____

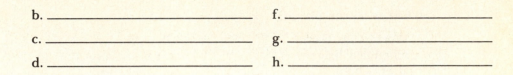

EXERCISE 1–1

Identifying Categories which Limit Topic Sentences

Directions: Notice the controlling words and phrases which have been underlined in the example sentence. They have also been identified as to type. Notice also that it is possible to have *more than one* category in a single topic sentence. After you have studied the example, do the same for the remaining sentences. Choose from the eight categories:

| 1. place | 3. quality | 5. differences | 7. effect |
| 2. time | 4. similarities | 6. number | 8. cause |

1. Soccer has become increasingly popular in the United States in the last ten years.   (quality)   (place)   (time)
2. Team sports develop an athlete's sense of fair play.
   (   )
3. Libraries have three basic kinds of materials.
   (   )
4. Women are paid less for equal work than men in certain U.S. companies.
   (   )   (   )
5. Pollution has caused three major problems in our town in the last five years.   (   ) (   ) (   ) (
)
6. Air travel is more convenient than train travel for at least three reasons.
   (   )   (   ) (   )

Before you actually begin to write a paragraph, it is usually a good idea to *plan* what you want to say about your general topic. One way to plan is to explore the topic by making a list of the things that come to your mind when you ask yourself questions about your topic. Using the topic *soccer* as an example, you might want to ask questions according to the categories we have already discussed.

Where is soccer played?

in Europe   in Asia
in Africa   in the U.S.

When is soccer played?

World Cup Games	Olympics
scheduled leagues	warm season
after school	on weekends

How can soccer be described?

fast	uniforms
players	dangerous
rules	popular
ball	field
plays	penalties

Is soccer similar to any other game?

American football
rugby
lacrosse

Is soccer different from these games?

yes—each in different ways

How many players are on a soccer team?

eleven

What are the effects of playing soccer?

athletic skill	good shape
admired by fans	publicity
sense of fair play	

Why do people play soccer?

fun
popular
good exercise

Of course, it would not be possible to write about all of the things on your list in one paragraph. Therefore, after you have compiled your list, you will want to select key words or phrases from your answers which seem to fit together logically. Usually, key words chosen from one to three categories will be adequate to limit your topic to the kind of information which can be developed in one paragraph. Notice that in the soccer example, we can choose from among the answers to our questions to formulate all of the topic sentences shown in the box on page 4.

Keep in mind that, depending on the general topic you are working with, it is not always possible to ask and answer questions in all of the categories. For instance, you probably would not want to ask whether smoking is similar to anything else. Likewise, you will probably use the number category only to place a limit on places, time, similarities, differences, causes, and effects.

EXERCISE 1–2

Guided Practice in Exploring Your Topic

Directions: Working alone or in small groups, make a list of all the possible answers you can think of to the following questions about a famous leader with whom you are familiar. Then, selecting key words and phrases from at least two categories, formulate two different topic sentences.

1. Where did he/she work, live, and die?
2. When did he/she live?
3. What kind of person was he/she? How did he/she look?
4. Was he/she similar to other leaders? How?
5. Was he/she different from other leaders? How?
6. What were the effects of his/her work?
7. Why is he/she well known?

EXERCISE 1–3

Exploring Your Topic

Directions: Working alone or in small groups, ask questions based on the categories about the following topics. All of the topics are too general to write about in one paragraph. After you have answered the questions, select key words or phrases for each topic from the categories. Then, for each topic, write *two* completely different topic sentences which might be developed into two completely different paragraphs. In parentheses beneath the topic sentences, indicate what categories you have used. Your topic sentences should look like those in the example.

Example:

Topic: Soccer

1. There are many reasons for soccer's increased popularity
           (number)   (description)
   in the United States.
       (place)
2. Latin Americans generally prefer soccer to football.
     (place)   (differences)

Choose a Topic

1. supermarkets
2. smoking
3. study habits
4. problems between generations
5. registration process at a university

EXERCISE 1–4

Writing Topic Sentences

Directions: Working alone, formulate questions about the following topic based on the categories. Then write *three* separate topic sentences about the topic. When you have finished, compare your sentences with those of some of your classmates to decide whether you have limited the topic adequately.

Topic: Foreign students in the United States

PARAGRAPH UNITY

Remember that besides the topic sentence, a paragraph includes several other sentences which in some way contribute to or *support* the idea in the topic sentence. In other words, all these sentences must be *related* to the topic and must therefore refer back to the topic sentence. Notice the arrows in the following diagram:

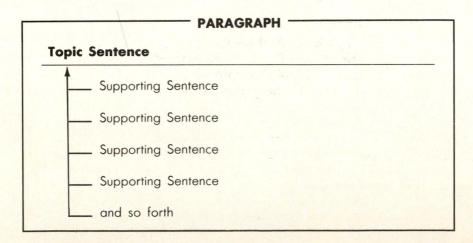

It is possible, of course, that some sentences may be directly related to the preceding supporting sentences (that is, they provide examples, details, or further explanation):

```
┌──────────────────── PARAGRAPH ────────────────────┐
│                                                    │
│  Topic Sentence                                    │
│  _____  │
│       ↑                                            │
│    ┌──── Supporting Sentence                       │
│    │         ↑                                      │
│    │      └─ Supporting Sentence                    │
│    │      └─ Supporting Sentence                    │
│    │                                                │
│    ├──── Supporting Sentence                       │
│    └──── and so forth                              │
│                                                    │
└────────────────────────────────────────────────────┘
```

❧ Now Ask Yourself

1. What must all supporting sentences do?_____

_____

2. What is illustrated by the arrows in the two previous diagrams?

(the first diagram)_____

_____

(the second diagram)_____

_____

If a paragraph does all this—that is, (1) if it announces its main idea in the topic sentence, and (2) if all the supporting sentences contribute to the reader's understanding of the main idea—we say that a paragraph is *unified*, or that it has *unity*. If the paragraph fails to do this, we say that it lacks unity.

Study the following paragraph. It *lacks* unity. Before reading the explanation which follows, can you figure out why it is not unified? (The sentences have been numbered only to make the discussion easier. Do not number sentences like this when you write a paragraph!)

[1]There are two main reasons why I have decided to attend Bingston University next year. [2]Applying to a college is a terribly complicated process. [3]Some of my friends chose colleges for

very bad reasons. [4]John has never been to college. [5]I've met his grandfather, and he still has an incredibly sharp mind for a man of his age. [6]Susan chose a university because the food in the region was said to be quite good. [7]Susan is really not too clever, I suppose, so I shouldn't criticize her. [8]Actually, I think it was her father who made the choice for her.

Did you notice that *none* of the preceding sentences actually discusses the topic which was announced in the topic sentence? The paragraph was supposed to be about the writer's *two main reasons* for choosing Bingston University. However, we are never told the reasons. The author mentions many unrelated things—his friend John, John's grandfather, his friend Susan, Susan's stupidity, and so forth—*but not the* **two** *reasons for choosing Bingston University!* If we wanted to show this by means of a diagram of the paragraph, we might do it this way:

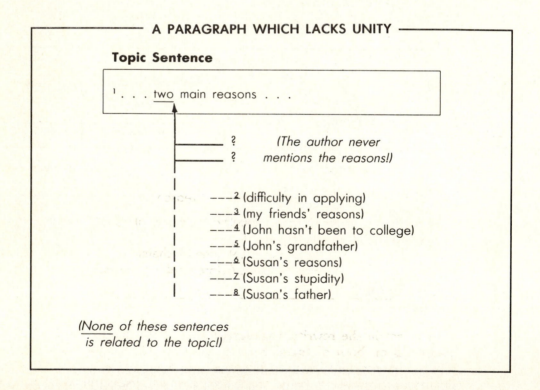

A PARAGRAPH WHICH LACKS UNITY

Topic Sentence

[1] . . . two main reasons . . .

? *(The author never*
? *mentions the reasons!)*

---[2] (difficulty in applying)
---[3] (my friends' reasons)
---[4] (John hasn't been to college)
---[5] (John's grandfather)
---[6] (Susan's reasons)
---[7] (Susan's stupidity)
---[8] (Susan's father)

(None of these sentences is related to the topic!)

If we wanted to keep the same topic sentence and rewrite the paragraph in a more unified fashion, we might end up with something like this:

[1]There are two main reasons why I have decided to attend Bingston University next year. [2]First of all, there is the question of money: Bingston's tuition is reasonable, and I don't even

have to pay it all at once. ³This is very important, since my father is not a rich man. ⁴With Bingston's deferred payment plan, my father will be able to pay my tuition without too much difficulty. ⁵The second reason is the fine education which I feel I will receive there in agriculture, my chosen field. ⁶It is a well-known fact that Bingston hires only the finest professors in its Agriculture Department. ⁷Moreover, the university requires all agricultural students to gain practical experience by working on local farms while they are still going to school.

This is what a diagram of the preceding paragraph would look like:

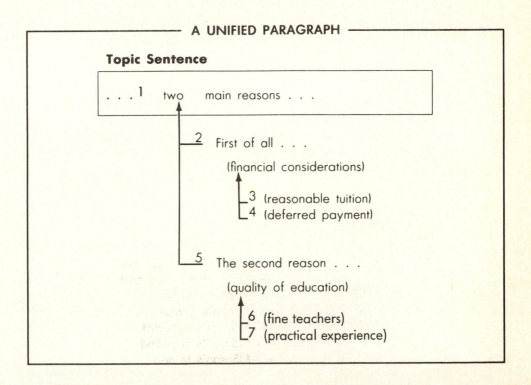

Notice that in the rewritten paragraph, the writer gives us *both* reasons and comments on both of them. Nothing is extra. Nothing is irrelevant to the topic announced in the topic sentence. *The paragraph is unified.* This means that the reader will have no trouble quickly understanding what the writer is trying to say.

☙ Now Ask Yourself

1. How are sentences 2 and 5 related to the topic sentence?_____

2. How are sentences 3 and 4 related to sentence 2?_____

3. How are sentences 6 and 7 related to sentence 5?_____

4. Why is the rewritten paragraph better than the original one?_____

EXERCISE 1–5

Identifying Irrelevant Sentences

Directions: The following paragraphs contain sentences which are not directly related to the main ideas of those paragraphs. Draw a line through the irrelevant sentence(s) of each paragraph. Then circle the *key words or phrases* in the topic sentence. Be prepared to explain why you think the sentences are irrelevant.

Example

1. _____ ¹(Different people) spend their weekends in (different ways.) ²Some enjoy going to the mountains to hike, ski, or just relax. ³Water skiing is much more difficult than snow skiing. ⁴Others prefer going to the beach to enjoy the seashore activities and to get a suntan. ⁵Some of these people work very hard during the week; others have rather relaxing jobs. ⁶Still others like to relax by staying home and reading a good book.

2. ¹Ever since the time of the Greeks, drama has played an important role in people's lives. ²The Greek tragedies and comedies were a central part of the life of the citizens of ancient Greece. ³During the Middle Ages, Bible stories were acted out in churches, and wandering companies of players performed in the streets. ⁴William Shakespeare lived during the Elizabethan period. ⁵The English language has changed somewhat since Shakespeare's time. ⁶In modern times, drama is brought directly into people's homes through the magic of television. ⁷Television also offers people such things as quiz and variety shows.

3.   [1]The general population often resists innovations, whether practical or aesthetic. [2]When the early experimenters in the field of aviation began their work, there were many who said, "If God had wanted man to fly, He would have given him wings." [3]The Wright brothers made the first powered flights in a heavier-than-air craft in 1903 at Kitty Hawk, North Carolina. [4]Even today there are many who strongly object to modern art and music as being nothing more than "splashes of paint and honking horns." [5]The painter Picasso's well-known masterpiece "The Three Musicians" is done primarily in blues and browns.

4.   [1]Zoos are popular with all children. [2]They are able to see examples of wildlife from all continents. [3]In wildlife pre-serves in Africa, the animals wander about freely without fear of being captured. [4]Perhaps the favorite spot in a zoo is the elephant cage. [5]There the elephants entertain the children by spraying themselves with their trunks and doing various tricks. [6]The children are especially delighted when an elephant takes peanuts from them with its trunk.

5.   [1]Editorials differ from other kinds of news stories. [2]In most regular news stories, it is assumed that no personal opinions are being represented. [3]Newspaper writers are supposed to present the facts of each story in a straight-forward, unbiased fashion. [4]Statistics reveal that over 61 million newspapers are sold every day in this county. [5]The purpose of the editorial page, of course, is to allow the editors to give their personal opinions. [6]Here is where they tell readers what they think about an issue—who is at fault, who has done a good job, or how a situation could be improved. [7]It is no wonder, then, that Thomas Jefferson once remarked that he could more easily accept newspapers without government than government without newspapers.

6.   [1]In order to find a suitable apartment, you must follow a very systematic approach. [2]First, you must decide which neighborhood would be most convenient for you. [3]Then you must determine how much rent your budget will allow. [4]Utility bills for houses average between $100 and $150 per month. [5]Your next step is to check the classified ads in the news-papers. [6]If you do not plan to buy furniture, you should check under "Apartments for rent—furnished." [7]Otherwise, check under "Apartments for rent—unfurnished." [8]In either case, however, be sure to check these ads regularly, since new listings appear each day. [9]After you have telephoned the apartments which seem likely choices, you must begin your long journey to inspect each one of them.

EXERCISE 1–6

Identifying Suitable Topic Sentences

Directions: After reading each of the following paragraphs, select the most suitable topic sentence from the three choices following it, and write the sentence which you have selected in the blank. Then try to explain why each of the other two items is not appropriate. Follow the example. Possible reasons for not choosing an item might be that:

It is too general.

It is too specific.

It is not a complete grammatical sentence.

It does not relate to the supporting sentences.

Example

I.   There are some minor differences between American and British spelling. Where Britons end certain words with *-se,* Americans usually end the same words with *-ce,* (British *practise* versus American *practice*); the reverse is sometimes true, too (British *defence* versus American *defense*). Notice also the British preference for final *-re* over the American *-er* (*metre* versus *meter*). Finally, most Americans consider *neighbor* a correct spelling, but a Briton characteristically adds a *u* and spells the word *neighbour.*

Choose a Topic Sentence

A. British and American English are not the same.
B. There are some minor differences between American and British spelling.
C. The endings of British and American words are not the same.

Defend Your Choice

1. I did not choose letter A because it is too general (some aspects are not the same; others are).
2. I did not choose letter C because it is too general (some endings are not the same).

II. _____

_____. The operation of both devices can be thought of as being divided into three phases: *input, processing,* and *output.* In the case of the computer, the information which is fed into the machine—the data—is the input; the internal operations of the machine constitute the processing; and the result—usually a printout—is called the output. The telephone, too, acts on information presented to it and produces a result. The input is the actual dialing of the number. The switching system which locates the number can be considered the processing phase. Finally, the telephone rings on the other end of the line, indicating that the call has been completed; this constitutes the output.[1]

Choose a Topic Sentence

A. Both the computer and the telephone are helpful inventions.
B. Computer terminology, such as *input* and *output,* is frequently used in other contexts.
C. Despite apparent differences, the operation of the computer and the telephone have much in common.

Defend Your Choice

1. I did not choose letter __ because_____

_____

2. I did not choose letter __ because_____

_____

III. _____

_____. The jack is a portable device for raising the car. It operates by means of force applied to a level on which the car is balanced. The lug wrench is a tool with a fixed "jaw" for gripping the lug (the type of screw used to hold a tire in place). It has a long handle so that it is effective in turning the lug, either to tighten or to loosen it. These two tools, which are necessary to change a tire, are usually found in the trunk of the car and are kept there at all times so that the motorist can use them in case of a flat tire.

[1] Adapted from John C. Keegel, *The Language of Computer Programming in English* (New York: Regents Publishing Co., Inc., 1976), p. 4.

Choose a Topic Sentence

A. Flat tires constitute a serious problem for the motorist.
B. How to change a flat tire.
C. The two tools necessary to change a tire are considered standard equipment on new U.S. automobiles.

Defend Your Choice

1. I did not choose letter ___ because_____

   _____

2. I did not choose letter ___ because_____

   _____

IV. _____

_____. The first one is the small pocket dictionary. Dictionaries of this type are usually only abridgments of earlier, more comprehensive dictionaries. The definitions found in a pocket dictionary are usually rather sketchy, and few or no example sentences are given to help the international student understand *how* the word is actually used in a sentence. Equally inadequate is the bilingual dictionary (Thai-English, Spanish-English, Russian-English, and so forth). This type of dictionary is often based on the idea of making word-for-word translations, a notion which shows no understanding of the idiomatic nature of all languages. Moreover, bilingual dictionaries are often hastily and sloppily compiled, as well as hopelessly out of date even before they are published.

Choose a Topic Sentence

A. A number of dictionaries are inappropriate for international students.
B. Some dictionaries aren't comprehensive enough.
C. The worst kind of dictionaries.

Defend Your Choice

1. I did not choose letter ___ because_____

   _____

2. I did not choose letter ___ because_____

   _____

V. _____

_____. In 1980, there were approximately 25 million Americans who were sixty-five or older. By the late 1980s, the number of these senior citizens had risen to over 30 million. This trend toward an increasingly older population, attributed largely to better health care, is expected to continue. In fact, the U.S. Census Bureau projects that the number of elderly Americans in the year 2020 will reach over 50 million, double the 1980 figure.

Choose a Topic Sentence

A. The population of older people in the United States has and will probably continue to increase rapidly.
B. The increasing population of senior citizens.
C. Health care in the United States is getting better for older people.

Defend Your Choice

1. I did not choose letter ___ because_____

_____

2. I did not choose letter ___ because_____

_____

VI. _____

_____. Infants usually satisfy this very basic need in the course of an ordinary day spent with their parents (feeding, kissing, bathing, and so forth). However, if a baby is neglected or even mistreated by being deprived of touch, his or her development will suffer on all levels—physical, intellectual, and emotional. Some children have even been known to die from this lack of tactile stimulation; many doctors think that many unexplained "crib deaths" are directly related to lack of touch and its various consequences. Children given up for adoption at a tender age and placed in poorly run orphanages, children brought up by unaffectionate parents, and children whose parents touch them only to beat them—all these types of children run the risk of never reaching their potential as fully developed adults.

Choose a Topic Sentence

A. Babies interacting daily with their parents.
B. Physical contact is an important factor in an infant's overall development.
C. Many children are not properly taken care of by their parents.

Defend Your Choice

1. I did not choose letter ___ because_____

_____

2. I did not choose letter ___ because_____

_____

EXERCISE 1–7

Supplying Appropriate Topic Sentences

Directions: The topic sentences of each of the following paragraphs have been omitted. After a *careful* reading, write an appropriate topic sentence for each. Notice that the *general topics* of these paragraphs are the same as those in the previous exercise.

1. 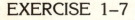 _____

_____. When you have removed the hubcap from the wheel which has the flat, correctly place the jack to lift the car off the ground. Now you are ready to jack up the car high enough for the tire to clear the ground. After you have done that, carefully loosen the nuts that hold the tire and rim in place; the tool you use to do that is called a *lug wrench.* Remove the tire and put the spare tire in place. Now you are ready to put the nuts back on the wheel and tighten them as firmly as you can with the lug wrench. All that remains is to replace the hubcap, lower the car to the ground, give the nuts a final tightening, and remove the jack.

2. _____

_____. The one most people are familiar with is the "desk dictionary," sometimes referred to as a *general-purpose dictionary.* Another kind is the *pronouncing dictionary,* which is concerned with a word's pronunciation more than with its meaning. A third type is the *bilingual dictionary,* which lists the words in one language and attempts to give equivalent meanings in another language. Other types include *technical dictionaries, special-purpose dictionaries,* and *scholarly dictionaries.*

3. _____

_____. Under this system, the customer's monthly telephone bill includes specific information for each long-distance call: the date and time of each call, the rate charged per minute (based on the company's discount system), the length of time the call took, the number and place called, whether the call was direct-dialed or operator-assisted, and the amount charged for the call. As each call is placed, all of this information is fed into a computer and programmed onto each customer's billing card, thus simplifying and clarifying the entire billing process. The telephone company hopes that its billing procedure will reduce the number of inquiries and free its employees to do work which computers are not yet able to perform.

4. _____

_____. Surveys indicate that Social Security benefits constitute the main source of income (about 37 percent) for retired Americans who are over sixty-five years of age. The Social Security system, which is a fund financed jointly by workers, employers, and the federal government, provides monthly payments to retired persons and pays for some of their medical bills. Earnings from part-time jobs account for approximately 25 percent of the income of retired Americans. Almost half of the retired population works on a part-time basis, and most do so at a lower salary than they earned before retirement. Assets, including property, stocks, and money saved during working years provide another 23 percent of retirement income. Surprisingly, money from pensions (retirement plans) supplies only 13 percent of retirees' total fiscal support. The remaining 2 percent is attributed to unspecified other sources.

5. _____

_____. It will teach you how to pronounce new words correctly. It will also show you the correct spellings of these words. Most dictionaries will then give you certain important grammatical information about each word—whether it is a noun or an adjective, for example, or how the past tense of a verb is spelled. Many dictionaries will also give the etymology of a word, telling you which language it originally came from. But perhaps most importantly, a dictionary tells you what a word means. Most words have several meanings, and a good dictionary helps you to understand the word in all its different meanings by giving you clear definitions and useful examples.

6. _____

_____. In some cultures, the act of touching another person is considered very intimate and is therefore reserved for people who know each other very well. In the United States, for example, young children are taught that it is rude to stand too close to people. By the time they are adults, Americans have learned to feel most comfortable when standing at about arm's length away from people to whom they are talking. And many Americans do not touch each other with great frequency while talking (this is particularly true of men). In contrast, other cultures have more relaxed rules regarding touching. For example, it is usual for friends—both men and women—to embrace each other when they meet. When they talk, they generally stand closer than Americans do, and they touch each other more often. They are as much at ease doing this as Americans are with more space between them, and they feel just as uncomfortable with Americans' "touching rules" as Americans feel with theirs.

7. _____

_____. First, with a word processor it is possible to type over a word or words that you want to change, while with a standard typewriter it is necessary either to erase or use correction fluid or tape and then type in the corrections. The second advantage is that you can add words or sentences in the middle of a paragraph and then command the computer to put your text back in proper paragraph form. When using a standard typewriter, the only way to add new information is to retype the entire paragraph. A third benefit of using a computer to write is that you can move entire paragraphs within longer papers simply by pushing a key. With a typed text, this can be accomplished only with scissors and paste, which produces sloppy-looking work.

*8. _____

_____. To begin with, this sense seems so essential to us that we have at least four common verbs in English to describe various ways of using our eyes. We can *look,* we can *glance* (look quickly and

---

* From this point on in the text, some items in some exercises will be marked with an asterisk to indicate that, because of vocabulary, length, or subject matter, they are more challenging.

then look away), we can *stare* (look for a long time, perhaps rudely), and we can *glare* (stare angrily). We sometimes equate this sense with intellectual understanding. When we understand what someone is saying, we might say, "I see what you mean." We also use the sense of sight in the opposite way—that is, to suggest lack of understanding. When we don't understand something, we say that we are "in the dark"; and in a situation which we cannot (and perhaps even stubbornly refuse to) understand, our friends might accuse us of being "blind to the truth." Lack of light (and therefore of sight as well) is sometimes even associated with unpleasant character traits: a *gloomy* person is too serious, and a particularly unpleasant person is said to have a "dark side" to his or her personality. The presence of light, however—whether applied to a person's character or to life in general—suggests hope and optimism. When we are feeling pessimistic about things, our friends remind us to "look on the bright side," or they comfort us with assurances that "every cloud has a silver lining."

SUPPORTING TOPIC SENTENCES

Examples, Details, Anecdotes, Facts and Statistics

Once you have limited your subject by writing a good topic sentence, you must next *develop* that subject so that the reader thoroughly understands what you mean to say. When you are speaking, you do this unconsciously, often by repeating yourself in different words and by using *gestures* and *facial expressions*. In writing, *you cannot make use of these auditory and visual aids,* so you must think and plan carefully what you are going to write to ensure that your reader knows exactly what you mean.

There are many ways in which you can develop and clarify a topic sentence. In this unit we will deal with four of these:

1. EXAMPLES
2. DETAILS
3. ANECDOTES
4. FACTS AND STATISTICS

Examples

An example is a *specific instance that explains a more general idea.* Red is an example of a color, the United States is an example of a country, a lemon is an example of a fruit, and so on. Because examples are specific (smaller, more limited, and often more concrete), they are often easier to understand than more general ideas, and perhaps that is why writers often use them.

Model Paragraph

Some of the most interesting words in English are the actual names of the people first involved in the activities suggested by the meanings of the words. The word *boycott,* for instance, derives from the case of Sir Charles Boycott (1832–97), a land agent in Ireland whose tenants ostracized him because he refused to lower their rents. Vidkun Quisling's name quickly became an infamous addition to the English language during World War II. He was a Norwegian politician who betrayed his country to the Nazis, and his name, *quisling,* is now synonymous with *traitor.* Perhaps a more common example is *Levis.* These popular blue jeans are named after Levi Strauss, the man who first manufactured them in San Francisco in 1850. Perhaps most omnipresent of all is the *sandwich,* named for the Fourth Earl of Sandwich (1718–92), who created this quick portable meal so that he would not have to leave the gambling table to eat. Other words in this unique category include *lynch, watt, davenport,* and *zeppelin.*

Now Ask Yourself ✍

1. What examples is the author giving?_____

2. How many examples are given?_____

3. Use an English dictionary to determine the meanings and origins of the following words: lynch, watt, davenport, zeppelin. Try to give a definition, a name, dates, and a brief description of the person associated with each word.

EXERCISE 2–1

Guided Analysis of the Use of Examples

Directions: Complete the analysis of the model paragraph by filling in all the blank spaces. Note that key phrases in the topic sentence have been circled.

ANALYSIS

Topic Sentence: Some of the (most interesting words) in English are the actual (names of the people) first involved in the activities suggested by the meanings of the words.

Example: boycott

Example: quisling

Example:

Example:

Example:

Example:

Example:

Example:

EXERCISE 2–2

Guided Analysis of the Use of Examples

Directions: Read and analyze the following paragraph.

In order to be considered a hero by his or her own and subsequent generations, a person must display extraordinary physical or intellectual powers. The physical hero—one who exhibits great strength to overcome monumental obstacles and emerge a victor—is frequently found in literature. Samson, although chained and bound, used his superhuman strength to destroy his enemies, the Philistines. Joan of Arc inspired the French army with her energy and willingness to share their hardships. Likewise, Dwight Eisenhower, a more contemporary physical hero, surmounted overwhelming odds to organize the successful Allied invasion of "Fortress Europe" during World War II. A second heroic type is the intellectual, admired for his or her mental prowess and the way he or she uses it to the benefit of mankind. Leonardo DaVinci, with his studies of architecture, human anatomy, and engineering, in addition to his great artistic achievements, is a perfect example of this second type. More recently, Madame Curie or Albert Einstein, who not only made far-reaching contributions in the physical sciences but also worked diligently toward achieving world peace, illustrate the intellectual hero.

ANALYSIS

> **Topic Sentence:**

Example (Physical Hero): _____

Example (Physical Hero): _____

Example (Physical Hero): _____

Example (   ): _____

Example (   ): _____

Example (   ): _____

STRUCTURES OF EXEMPLIFICATION

If writers wish to do so, they can remind their readers that they are giving examples by using *signal* words or phrases. Using one of these signals is like saying to the reader, "Pay attention; now I am giving you an example." Most writers do not use a signal every time they give an example. When many examples are given, it is often enough to give only one or two signals; or a writer may decide that the paragraph is so easy to understand that no signal is necessary.

When a writer decides to use a signal, it can appear either in the *same* sentence as the general idea or in the sentence(s) following the general idea.

Group I. Noun and Verb Signals

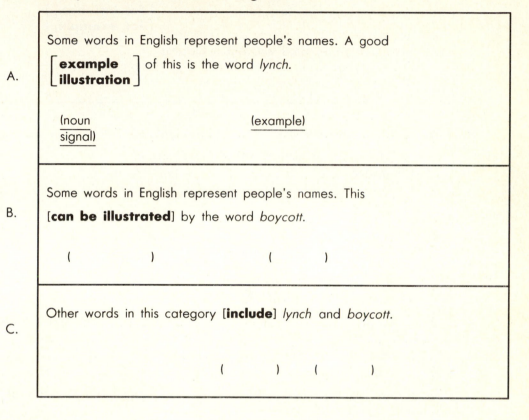

A.
Some words in English represent people's names. A good

⎡**example**   ⎤ of this is the word *lynch.*
⎣**illustration**⎦

(noun
signal)   (example)

B.
Some words in English represent people's names. This

[**can be illustrated**] by the word *boycott.*

(   )   (   )

C.
Other words in this category [**include**] *lynch* and *boycott.*

(   ) (   )

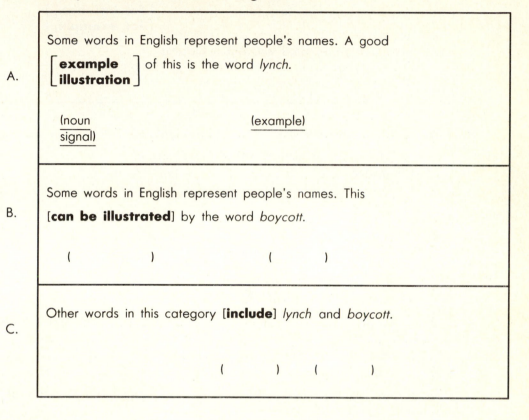 Now Ask Yourself

1. What kind of signal—noun or verb—is shown in box B? (Fill in the parentheses.)
2. What kind of signal is shown in box C? (Fill in the parentheses.)

Group II. Sentence Connectors

These are words and phrases used to join *two complete grammatical sentences.* A semicolon (;) is often used before a sentence connector. However, since each of the sentences can stand alone and be considered grammatically correct, a period (.) can also be used after the first sentence. In either case, a comma (,) is used *after* the sentence connector.

A.

> Some English words represent proper names. [For instance, / For example,]
>
> the word *quisling* originated with Vidkun Quisling.
>
> (   )   (   )

B.

> Some English words represent proper names. The word *quisling*,
>
> [for example, / for instance,]   originated with Vidkun Quisling.
>
> (   )   (   )

Now Ask Yourself

1. What are the sentence connectors, and what are the examples? (Fill the parentheses.)
2. What difference in meaning is there between *for example* and *for instance*?

   _____

3. What punctuation is used to separate the signal from the rest of the sentence?

   _____

   Why does this punctuation come both before and after the signals in box B?_____

4. Rewrite the sentence from either box A or box B by using a semicolon (;).

   _____

   _____

5. Rewrite the sentence in box A by using a signal from Group 1.

   Some English words _____. A good

   _____ *quisling,* which _____.

Group III. Phrase Signals

A phrase (a group of words) is not a complete sentence; it is *part* of a sentence.

A.

Words ⎡ **like**   ⎤ *lynch* and *quisling* represent proper names.
        ⎣ **such as** ⎦

(   ) (   )

B.

[**Such** words **as**] *lynch* and *quisling* represent proper names.

(   )   (   )

C.

Some words represent proper names. *Lynch* is [**such a**] word.

or: . . . *Lynch* and *quisling* are [**such**] words.

(   ) (   )

❧ Now Ask Yourself

1. What are the examples, and what are the phrase signals? (Fill in the parentheses.)
2. Which of the signals in box A can be written in more than one way?___

_____

3. In box C, when would you use *such a,* and when would you use *such?*___

_____

4. Rewrite the sentence from box C using a semicolon.

_____

❧ ─────────────────────────────────────   EXERCISE 2–3

Joining Phrases and Sentences of Exemplification

Directions: For each of the following items, mark the example(s) by writing X in the correct blank. Then, combine the items in the suggested way.

Example:

1. _____ Some words in English represent people's names.

   __X__ The word *quisling* comes from the name of a Norwegian politician.

   (for instance) Some words in English represent people's names. The word
   quisling, for instance, comes from the name of a Norwegian politician.

   (For instance could start the second sentence, and a semicolon could be
   used instead of a period between the two sentences.)

2. _____ Some articles of clothing were named for the people who invented
   them.

   _____ The word *mackintosh* (a kind of raincoat) takes its name from
   Charles Macintosh, a Scottish inventor.

   (for example) _____

   _____

3. _____ The verb *to lynch* (to hang someone illegally by mob action)
   probably originated with Captain William Lynch, an eighteenth-
   century Virginian.

   _____ Some words are the actual names of the people first involved in
   the activities suggested by the meanings of those words.

   (a good illustration of this) _____

   _____

4. _____ DaVinci and Einstein

   _____ Intellectual heroes used their intelligence for the good of mankind.

   (such as) _____

   _____

5. _____ Occasionally a literary character adds a new word to the English
   language.

   _____ The Spanish character Don Quixote gave us the word *quixotic*
   (extravagantly romantic or impractical).

   (can be illustrated) _____

   _____

6. _____ *for example* or *for instance*

   _____ When writers want to give examples, they sometimes announce
   these examples with signals.

(like) _____

_____

7. _____ The zeppelin takes its name from Count Ferdinand von Zeppelin.

_____ Sometimes an invention becomes known by the name of its inventor.

(for instance) _____

_____

8. _____ Some people, through their bad deeds, live on in the language long after they have died.

_____ Vidkun Quisling was a Norwegian politician who betrayed his country.

(such a person) _____

_____

9. _____ _zeppelin_ and _mackintosh_

_____ An invention sometimes becomes known by the name of its inventor.

(such. . .as) (good examples of the fact that) ____

_____

The Paragraph in an Academic Setting: Answering Essay Questions[1]

All college or university students soon discover that the ability to write well-organized paragraphs is not just "something that you do in an English course." As a matter of fact, it serves another rather different function as well: passing _essay examinations._ Unlike objective exams (multiple choice, true-false, and so forth), essay exams require students to write longer answers _in paragraph form._ Some longer questions may even require several-paragraph answers.

How do you write a good answer to an essay question? There is no perfect formula that you can use in all situations, but your chances of passing this kind of exam will be greatly improved if you follow some simple guidelines:

1. Start by making a **general statement** (in other words, a topic sentence)

[1] If you are not in an academic program, skip over this section. In the writing assignments, choose the General Topics rather than the Academic Topics.

which contains **the main idea of the question.** Your topic sentence can even repeat key words and phrases found in the question.

2. Continue by **supporting** your topic sentence with **the kinds of information suggested in the question.** If the question asks for examples, give some. If it requires a physical description, write one. If statistics are required, provide them.

Consider the case of an essay exam question which asks for *examples* as part of the answer. Notice how the following sample answer starts with a general statement that seems to echo the main idea of the question.

> **QUESTION:** Give several examples of English words that are derived from the names of the people first involved in the activities suggested by the meanings of the words. Be sure to explain carefully the origins of the words you choose; no credit will be given for a word that is listed but not explained.

> **ANSWER:**

> Many English words are derived from the names of the people first involved in the activities suggested by the meanings of the words. The word *boycott,* for instance,_____

> _____

> _____ Another interesting example is the word *sandwich,* which_____

> _____

> _____

> _____ Other words in this same category include

> _____

> _____

EXERCISE 2–4

Exploring Your Topic

Directions: Choose one of the topics below and formulate questions about it based on the categories on page 4. Select key words and phrases from your list of answers and write a topic sentence for your paragraph. If you are working with a partner or in a group, show your topic sentence to some of your classmates to see if you have limited your topic sufficiently for one paragraph.

General Topics

the behavior of someone in love
watching television
owning a car

Academic Topics

Describe and give examples of the way English has influenced (your language).
What are the qualities a good student should possess?
What are the major exports of (your country)?

Note: If you choose an academic topic, write in an *objective* way. That is, use *Korean* or *Spanish* instead of *your language* in the first topic, or *Nigeria* or *Indonesia* for the third. Do not use personal pronouns, such as *I* or *my*.

EXERCISE 2–5

Paragraph Writing: Examples

Directions: Using the topic sentence you wrote in the previous exercise, write the first draft of a paragraph in which you use *examples* for support. When you have finished your paragraph, you may wish to show it to a classmate to see if the examples you have used develop your topic sentence clearly.

EXERCISE 2–6

Making Your Language Accurate

Directions: After you have revised your paragraph based on your classmates' suggestions, you will want to check it for correct usage. One of the most common errors that learners of English make is *subject-verb* agreement. Notice the examples of this kind of error in the following sentences.

Perhaps a more common example, at least among young
is
people around the world, ~~are~~ Levis.

In this sentence, the verb *are* does not agree with its subject. The subject of the verb is *example*, which is a singular noun. The correct verb is **is**.

> include
> Other words in this unique category ~~includes~~ *lynch, watt, davenport,* and *zeppelin.*

In this sentence, the verb *includes* does not agree with its subject. The subject of the verb is *words*, which is plural. The correct verb is **include.**

Proofread the sentences in your paragraph to make sure that the subjects and verbs agree. After you have corrected any errors, recopy this draft of your paragraph and submit it to your teacher.

Details

A detail is *a particular part or characteristic of a whole thing or a whole idea.* Details are frequently used in a description.

EXERCISE 2–7

Guided Analysis of the Use of Details

Directions: Analyze the paragraph below filling in the blanks in the chart that follows:

Model Paragraph

> Landlords usually require a renter to sign a very complicated contract called a *lease.* It stipulates the length of time the person must stay in the apartment and the amount of rent he or she must pay. It can limit the number of people allowed to live in the apartment and restrict the renter from having pets. A lease may prohibit the renter from subletting and include a provision by which the renter is charged a certain amount of money if he or she breaks the contract. The agreement also includes the responsibilities of the landlord, such as providing adequate heat, garbage removal, and exterior maintenance of the apartment building.

Topic Sentence: Landlords usually require a renter to sign a very (complicated contract) called (a lease.)

Detail: length of time

Detail:

Detail:

Detail:

Detail:

Detail:

Detail:

example: heat

example:

example:

EXERCISE 2–8

Analyzing the Use of Details

Directions: Read and analyze the following paragraph. In your choice of major categories of details for the diagram, you might want to consider number of rows, method of replacement, maximum number of teeth, and shape of the bite.

Perhaps it is because of its terrifying and effective teeth that the shark has always been one of man's most hated and feared enemies. Located beneath its snout, the shark's mouth contains between four and six rows of teeth, but these may number up to twenty-four rows in some species. The teeth are embedded in the gums and gradually move forward as they are used. Eventually, these large teeth drop out and are replaced by new teeth moving up from behind them. It is possible for one species of shark to produce up to 24,000 teeth over a ten-year period. This awesome dental equipment produces a jagged crescent-shaped bite.

ANALYSIS

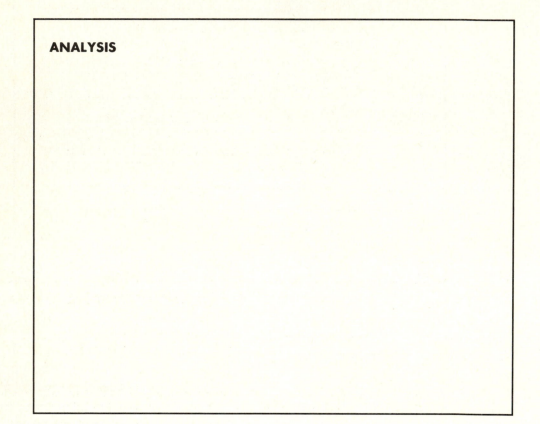

EXERCISE 2–9

Information Transfer (Details)

Directions: Write a paragraph based on the following diagram. Use the topic sentence which has been given. Be careful: The details are given in *note form*, so you will have to convert them into grammatical sentences.

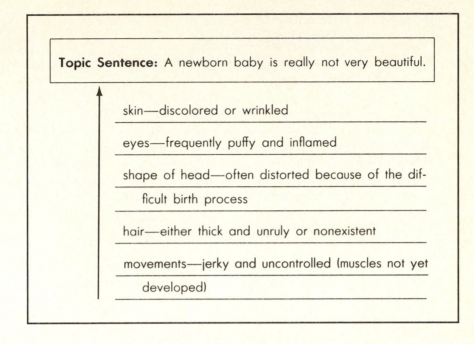

Topic Sentence: A newborn baby is really not very beautiful.

skin—discolored or wrinkled

eyes—frequently puffy and inflamed

shape of head—often distorted because of the difficult birth process

hair—either thick and unruly or nonexistent

movements—jerky and uncontrolled (muscles not yet developed)

EXERCISE 2–10

Paragraph Writing: Details

Phase 1: Exploring Your Topic

Directions: Choose one of the following topics and formulate questions about it based on the categories on page 4. Select key words and phrases from your answers and write a topic sentence. If you are working with a partner or in a group, show your topic sentence to your classmates to see if you have limited your topic sufficiently for one paragraph.

General Topics

the physical appearance of your favorite actor or actress
the characteristics of a good hospital nurse
the features you would like on your next car

Essay Questions

What are the legal rights of citizens in (your country)?

Describe the architecture of (a place in your country).
Describe the perfect study environment.

Note: Follow the directions for essay questions given in Exercise 2–5; that is, write objectively.

Phase 2: Writing the First Draft

Directions: Using the topic sentence you wrote in Phase 1, write the first draft of a paragraph in which you use *details* for support. When you have finished your paragraph, you may wish to show it to classmates to see if the details you have used develop your topic sentence clearly.

Phase 3: Making Your Language Accurate

Directions: After you have revised your paragraph based on your classmates' suggestions, you will want to check it for correct usage. Proofread the sentences to make sure that the **subjects** and **verbs** agree. After you have corrected any errors, recopy this draft and submit it to your teacher.

EXERCISE 2–11

Paragraph Writing: Details

Phase 1: Exploring Your Topic

Directions: Choose one of the following topics and formulate questions about it based primarily on the **description** category. Select key words and phrases from your answers and write a topic sentence. If you choose the general topic, do not show your topic sentence to anyone else in the class.

General Topic

Write a description of one of your classmates. Your teacher will give you time in class to take notes. Concentrate on the physical characteristics, such as height, weight, hair color, complexion, and so forth, not on clothing. Using the chart at the end of this exercise will help you with your description.

Essay Question

Write a description of an unusual animal which is found in your country. You may want to work from a picture of

this animal. Concentrate on the physical characteristics which
make this animal unique.

Don't Forget: Even in this kind of paragraph, the details you choose must support the topic sentence you have written.

Phase 2: Writing the First Draft

Directions: Using the topic sentence you wrote in Phase 1, write the first draft of a paragraph in which you use *details* to support your topic sentence. When you have finished, read your paragraph to your classmates *but do not read the name of the person or animal you are describing.* If your paragraph contains enough detail, your classmates will be able to guess who or what you have described. If it does not contain enough detail and your classmates cannot identify the person or animal, they can suggest ways for you to improve your description.

Phase 3: Making Your Language Accurate

Directions: After you have revised your paragraph based on your classmates' suggestions, you will want to check it for correct usage. Proofread the sentences to make sure that the **subjects** and **verbs** agree. After you have corrected any errors, recopy this draft and submit it to your teacher.

Describing a Person

SIZE

    X is about   _____'_____" tall.
            approximately

    X is tall.
            short
            of medium height
            thin
            slender
            a little on the heavy side
            average-sized

EYES, HAIR, AND SKIN

    X has brown eyes.   *X* is brown-eyed.
            blue   blue-eyed
            black   and so forth
            gray
            green
            dark
            light

X has black hair.	*X* is a blonde.
brown	a redhead
blonde	(Only these two!)
red	
gray	
dark	
light	
curly	
straight	
long	
short	
medium-length	
X has a light complexion.	*X* is light-skinned.
dark	dark-skinned
fair	freckled
freckled	
smooth	
tanned	
clear	

OTHER CHARACTERISTICS

X wears glasses.	*X* is attractive.
a wig	clean-shaven
	and so forth
X has a mustache.	
a beard	
a small nose	
freckles	
high cheekbones	

ANECDOTES

An anecdote is *a short, entertaining account of some happening*. It is usually *personal*. It may be thought of as *a lengthy example*.

Model Paragraph

Physical gestures and body language have different meanings in different cultures, and misunderstanding these signals can sometimes be embarrassing. Although I had spent a lot of time among non-Americans, I had never really realized what this could mean in practical terms. I had an experience which taught me well, however. Some years ago, I organized and accompanied a small group of visiting foreign students to New York for four days of sightseeing by bus. Because these students were rather young, and because New York is such an overwhelming city, I was constantly counting heads to be sure we hadn't lost anyone. In the U.S., it is very common to count people or things by pointing the index finger and, of course, I used this method. One young man became extremely quiet and pensive, and I thought that perhaps he wasn't enjoying himself. When I asked him what was the matter, he replied, "In my country, we count people with our eyes. We use our fingers to count the pigs."

ANALYSIS

> **Topic Sentence:** Physical gestures and body language have different meanings in different cultures, and misunderstanding these signals can sometimes be embarrassing.

↑

ANECDOTE: (the entire paragraph)

EXERCISE 2–12

Paragraph Writing: Anecdotes

Phase 1: Exploring Your Topic

Directions: In this exercise, topic sentences have been provided for you. After reading the topic sentences, select the one for which you can think of an appropriate anecdote. Share your anecdote with one of your classmates to see if it supports the topic sentence you have chosen.

General Topic Sentences

A person's life can sometimes change overnight.
Computers can create more problems than they solve.
Not knowing a language well can sometimes be embarrassing.

You know who your real friends are when you have a problem.
Love is not always happy.

Note: Anecdotes are generally not used to support academic topics.

Phase 2: Writing the First Draft

Directions: Using the topic sentence you have selected, write the first draft of a paragraph in which you use an *anecdote* for support. You may wish to show your paragraph to a different classmate for another opinion on whether your anecdote develops the topic sentence you have chosen.

Phase 3: Making Your Language Accurate

Directions: After you have revised your paragraph based on your classmate's suggestions, you will want to check it for correct usage. Proofread the sentences to make sure that the **subjects** and **verbs** agree. After you have corrected any errors, recopy this draft and submit it to your teacher.

FACTS AND STATISTICS

A fact is something which is objectively verifiable.

A statistic is *a numerical fact* which presents significant information about a given subject.

Model Paragraph

> The term *population explosion* is usually applied to the rapid growth of the last three centuries. In the 200 years from 1650 to 1850, world population doubled and reached its first billion. In the next 80 years, it doubled again; and by 1975, it had doubled once more to a total of 4 billion. At the beginning of the twenty-first century, it is estimated that it will exceed 6 billion and possibly approach 8 billion unless there is a major reduction in birth rates or a major increase in death rates.

EXERCISE 2–13

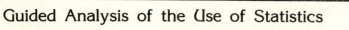

Guided Analysis of the Use of Statistics

Directions: Analyze the model paragraph above by filling in all the blank spaces in the diagram that follows.

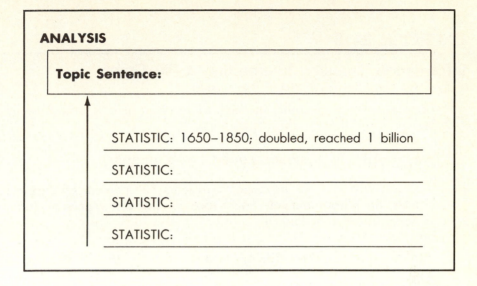

ANALYSIS

Topic Sentence:

STATISTIC: 1650–1850; doubled, reached 1 billion

STATISTIC:

STATISTIC:

STATISTIC:

EXERCISE 2–14

Analyzing the Use of Statistics

Directions: Read and analyze the following paragraph.

Exams apparently have a marked effect on the blood pressure of the students taking them. In a recent study, it was shown that the average student's blood pressure rose from 115/55 before the exam to 155/115 at the end of the exam. Ten minutes after the examination period had ended, the students' blood pressures were still quite high, averaging 150/110.

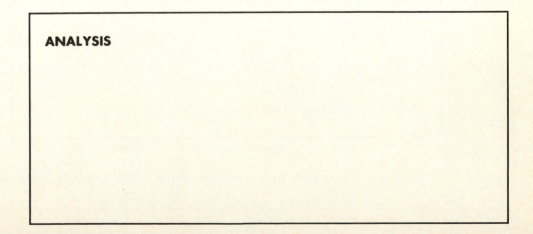

ANALYSIS

EXERCISE 2–15

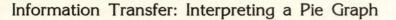

Information Transfer: Interpreting a Pie Graph

Directions: Working alone, in pairs, or in small groups, study the graph and answer the following study questions.

Pie Graphs (sometimes called *circle graphs*).

In this graph, the pie, or circle, represents 100 percent of a typical average elderly household budget. Each slice of the pie represents one type of expenditure in that budget.

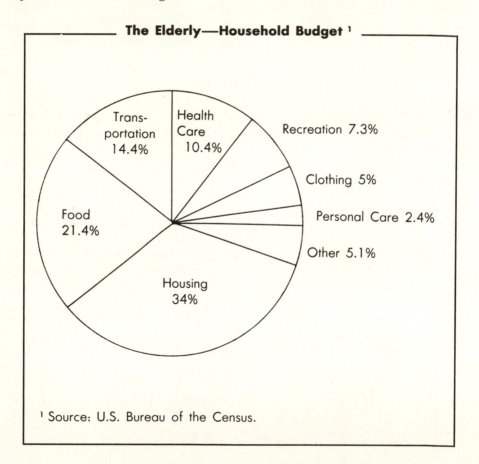

The Elderly—Household Budget [1]

[1] Source: U.S. Bureau of the Census.

1. What is the largest item in the budget of the average elderly household?

What is the next largest type of expenditure? _____

What is the smallest part of the budget? _____

2. About what percentage of the budget is spent on clothing? _____

3. Does the category *recreation* include transportation? _____

   How do you know? _____

4. Housing constitutes about one- _____ of the budget, and food represents about one- _____ . (Choose: half, third, fourth, or fifth.)

EXERCISE 2–16

Guided Paragraph Writing: Information Transfer

Phase 1: Exploring Your Topic

Directions: In this exercise, the topic sentence has been provided. After reading it, discuss the graph with one of your classmates to decide what kind of statistical evidence should be included to support the topic sentence. You may want to refer back to the study questions in Exercise 2–15 for ways to express your thoughts.

Topic Sentence

The average elderly household spends over three-fourths of its budget on the necessities of life.

Phase 2: Writing the First Draft

Directions: Using the suggested topic sentence, write the first draft of a paragraph in which you use statistical evidence for support. Arrange your statistics from the largest expenditure to the smallest. You may wish to show your paragraph to a different classmate for another opinion on whether the evidence that you have chosen develops the topic sentence clearly.

Phase 3: Making Your Language Accurate

Directions: After you have revised your paragraph based on your classmate's suggestions, you will want to check it for correct usage. Proofread the sentences to make sure that the **subjects** and the **verbs** agree. After you have corrected any errors, recopy this draft and submit it to your teacher.

EXERCISE 2–17

Paragraph Writing: Statistics

Phase 1: Exploring Your Topic

Directions: After reading the following essay question, discuss the pie graph with one of your classmates to decide what topic sentence should begin the answer and what kind of statistical evidence should support the topic sentence.

Essay Question

What are the various sources of income for the average senior citizen? Account for all sources and indicate percentages.

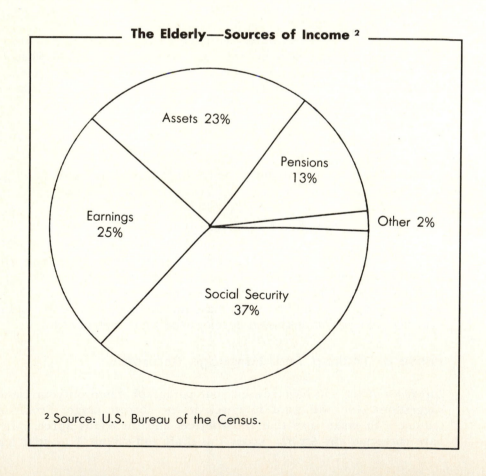

The Elderly—Sources of Income [2]

Assets 23%

Pensions 13%

Other 2%

Earnings 25%

Social Security 37%

[2] Source: U.S. Bureau of the Census.

Phase 2: Writing the First Draft

Directions: Using the topic sentence you have selected, write the first draft of a paragraph in which you use statistics for support. You may wish to show your paragraph to a different classmate for another opinion on whether your topic sentence seems clearly related to the question and whether the supporting sentences clearly develop the topic sentence.

Phase 3: Making Your Language Accurate

Directions: After you have revised your paragraph based on your classmate's suggestions, you will want to check it for correct usage. Proofread the sentences to make sure that the **subjects** and **verbs** agree. After you have corrected any errors, recopy this draft and submit it to your teacher.

3

ENUMERATION

Enumeration

Thus far, you have learned how to limit your subject in a clear, concise topic sentence and then to support it with examples, details, anecdotes, facts, and statistics. The next step is to arrange your supporting sentences in a logical and cohesive manner.

There are several ways in which this can be done. In this unit we will deal with what is probably the most common method of paragraph development in English: *enumeration*.

What is *enumeration?*

In this type of paragraph development, a writer starts with a *general class*, then proceeds to break it down by *listing* some *or* all *of its members or parts*. If we wanted to show a diagram of the enumerative process, our diagram might look something like this:

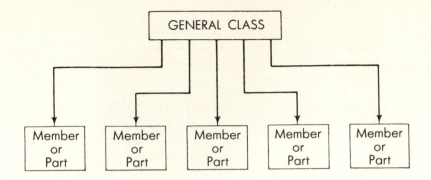

Model Paragraph

There are three basic kinds of materials that can be found in any good library. First, there are books on all subjects, both in English and in many other languages. These books are organized according to subject, title, and author in a central file called the *card catalog*. Books can generally be checked out of the library and taken home for a period of two to four weeks. Second, there are reference works, which include encyclopedias, dictionaries, bibliographies, atlases, and so forth, and which generally must be used in the library itself. Third, there are periodicals—magazines, newspapers, pamphlets—which are filed alphabetically in racks, or which have been microfilmed to conserve space. Like reference works, periodicals usually cannot be removed from the library.

Now Ask Yourself

1. What are the key words in the topic sentence of the model paragraph?

   _____

2. What types of supportive information does the author use (examples, details, anecdotes, facts and statistics)?_____

   _____

3. How many kinds or types of library materials are discussed?_____

4. What is meant by enumeration?_____

EXERCISE 3–1

Guided Analysis of Enumeration

Directions: Analyze the model paragraph by filling in the empty parts of the chart that follows.

> **Topic Sentence:** There are three basic kinds of materials that can be found in any good library.

KINDS OR TYPES	DESCRIPTION / EXAMPLES / ETC.
1. Books	On all subjects, in many languages; organized in the card catalog; usually can be checked out
2. Reference works	

ENUMERATORS

Notice the use of the word *kinds* in the preceding model paragraph. We will call this word an *enumerator,* since it helps us show the reader exactly what we are listing or enumerating. In the model paragraph, it is *kinds of materials.* Remember that enumerators are valuable key words. You should try to put them in the topic sentences of enumerative paragraphs. This will help you to organize your paragraphs more clearly; it will also help the reader to follow your train of thought more easily.

Writers frequently wish to make a list of other things besides *kinds* or *types.* They may, for example, want to talk about

classes	factors	divisions
parts	characteristics	subdivisions
elements	aspects	categories

LISTING SIGNALS

When making a list, people often use *numerals* (for example, 1, 2, 3, and so forth) to indicate the various items in the list. A simple list of this kind could be made for a model paragraph on library materials:

KINDS OF LIBRARY MATERIALS FOUND IN MOST GOOD LIBRARIES:

1. books
2. reference works
3. periodicals

In most formal writing, however, a list is not usually made with numerals.[1] The items are indicated by what we call *listing signals*. The author of the model paragraph has used three of these listing signals: *First, . . .; Second, . . .;* and *Third, ...* There are two main groups of listing signals in English. You should become very familiar with the words in these two groups.

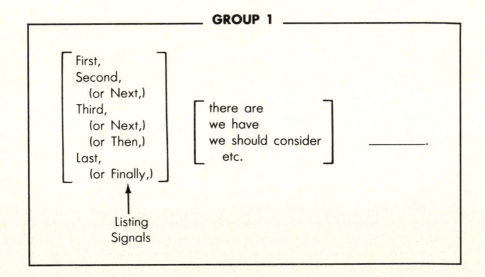

GROUP 1

First,
Second,
  (or Next,)
Third,
  (or Next,)
  (or Then,)
Last,
  (or Finally,)

↑
Listing
Signals

there are
we have
we should consider
  etc.

_____.

---

[1] A major exception to this is *scientific* and *technical* English, where it is common to find lists with a numeral before each item on the list.

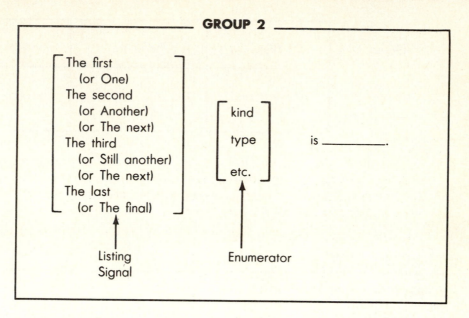

Now Ask Yourself

1. What is the difference between an enumerator and a listing signal?

_____

_____

2. What is another way to say each of the following?

   (Last,)_____

   (The final kind)_____

   (Another kind)_____

   (Next,)_____

3. What element does a Group 2 sentence have that a Group 1 sentence

   does not?_____

GROUP 1 VERSUS GROUP 2: SENTENCE STRUCTURE

There is one thing that you *must* remember. The words in Group 1 require a *different sentence structure* than the words in Group 2. Let's take a sentence from the model paragraph on library materials and illustrate this difference, which is really very simple:

Group 1:	First,	there are	books.
Group 2:	The first kind	$\begin{bmatrix} \text{is} \\ \text{consists of} \end{bmatrix}$	books.

Note that a full sentence follows the listing signals from Group 1. Notice also that in Group 2, the listing signal and enumerator are the subject of the sentence. These differences, although simple, are *very important!*

EXERCISE 3–2

Paraphrasing Listing Signals

Directions: Rewrite each of the following sentences in three ways, choosing words from *both* groups of listing signals. *Circle the enumerator* if you have used one.

1. Still another kind is periodicals.

   a. The next (kind) is periodicals. _____

   b. _____

   c. _____

2. Last, there are reference works.

   a. _____

   b. _____

   c. _____

EXERCISE 3–3

Supplying Listing Signals

Directions: Write listing signals for the following paragraph. Circle the enumerator in the topic sentence.

The science of proxemics has identified four main distances
at which Americans interact with each other. Each of these zones

has a close and distant phase. _____ the *intimate zone.* The close phase of this zone—actual physical contact to about 6 inches—is used only with our loved ones in such private activities as patting a child on the head or kissing. The distant phase—6 to 18 inches—is appropriate for very close friends but not for casual acquaintances. _____ the *personal zone.* Its close phase is roughly 18 inches to 2.5 feet, the distance family members stand from each other. The distant phase, which extends to about 4 feet, is common in a conversation among friends. _____ the *social zone,* which is typical of business dealings. Colleagues at work use close social distance (4 to 7 feet). The distant phase (7 to 12 feet) is automatically adopted in more formal circumstances—for example, when newly introduced people are assessing each other, or when a low-level employee is called into the boss's office. _____ the *public zone,* which is used on the most formal public occasions. The more important the speaker is, the further people stand from him or her. This zone can extend to 25 feet and beyond.

EXERCISE 3–4

Analyzing an Enumerative Paragraph

Directions: Fill in the following chart, which is based on the model paragraph in Exercise 3–3.

> **Topic Sentence:** The science of proxemics has identified four main distances or zones—each having a close and a distant phase—at which Americans interact with each other.

ZONE	PHASES, DISTANCES	USES
1. Intimate	The near phase (physical contact to six inches)	

ZONE	PHASES, DISTANCES	USES
2.		
3.		
4.		

Ascending Versus Descending Order

Thus far, the paragraphs in this unit have been structured so that all their parts are *of equal importance.* Thus, in the sample paragraph on library materials (page 50), no kind of library material is presented as being more important than any other kind; the paragraph represents, as we have already said, a simple, straightforward list.

The same thing can be said of the paragraph which talks about the writer's two main reasons for attending Bingston University (page 10.) If you remember, there was nothing in the paragraph to suggest that one reason was considered any more important than the other. The paragraph below also represents a simple list:

MY TWO MAIN REASONS FOR ATTENDING BINGSTON UNIVERSITY

1. Reasonable tuition; the deferred payment plan (financial reasons)
2. Fine teachers; practical work experience (academic reasons)

Sometimes, however, a writer wishes to indicate that one of the items in a list should receive special attention. In other words, the writer feels that one item is *more important, more interesting, more influential, stronger, bigger,* or *more basic* than the other items on the list. There are two ways in which an item can be singled out in a written paragraph: *ascending* and *descending* order.

DESCENDING ORDER

In *descending order,* the writer lists the most important point *first,* then goes on to speak of the other points. The writer usually thinks that the other points are important, too, but simply wishes to mention the most important one first.

Some writers like to imagine descending order in the shape of a *triangle with its base at the top.* This kind of triangle is bigger (more important) at the top and gets smaller (less important) as you move to the bottom.

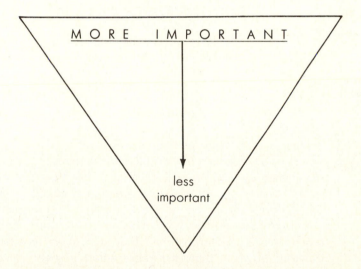

In a simple list using numerals, the most important item in the list can easily be indicated by drawing a circle or an arrow, by underlining, or by all three at the same time—anything to *catch the reader's eye.* In a written paragraph, however, we cannot do this. We indicate descending order by means of a special group of listing signals:

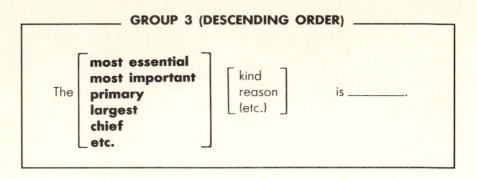

Let us illustrate the difference between a *list* in descending order and a *paragraph* in descending order. We will take the subject of Bingston University once again. This time, let us say that there are four reasons why the writer wants to attend Bingston University: its reasonable tuition, its deferred tuition plan, its work/study program, and its fine teachers. We will also assume that it is the *work/study program* that really attracts the writer to Bingston. A list which says all this might look something like the following:

MY REASONS FOR CHOOSING BINGSTON

1. Its work/study program
2. Its fine teachers
3. Its deferred payment plan
4. Its reasonable tuition

In paragraph form, the information might look like this:

There were several reasons why I decided to attend Bingston University. My chief reason for choosing that university was its wonderful work/study program in agriculture, my chosen field. The university requires all its agriculture students to gain practical experience by working on local farms while they are still going to school; I knew that this would provide invaluable experience and prepare me to better use the skills I had learned in the classroom. Second, Bingston hires only the finest teachers to teach in its graduate program. Then, too, there was Bingston's deferred payment plan; this represented a great convenience to my parents. A final reason was the reasonable tuition.

ASCENDING ORDER

Ascending order is exactly the *opposite* of descending order. In ascending order, we list the minor points first, *saving the most important for last*. This keeps the reader interested, since the paragraph has a kind of dramatic structure to it: it builds up to or ascends to a climax.

Just as a triangle was used to illustrate descending order, we can use a triangle to show how ascending order works. However, this time the base of the triangle is on the bottom.

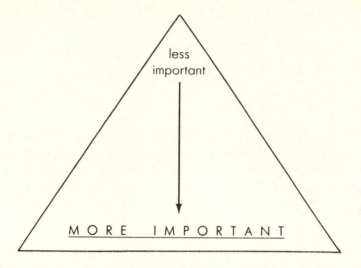

The listing signals used for ascending order are really the same as those used for descending order: the writer states that the last item is the most important, the largest, etc. If writers really want to emphasize this importance, they can do this in several ways:

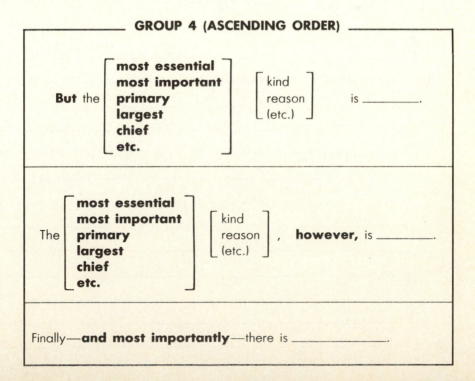

Going back to the subject of Bingston University, the list of the writer's reasons for attending that university can now be rewritten in ascending order. The list would look something like this:

MY REASONS FOR CHOOSING BINGSTON

1. Its reasonable tuition
2. Its deferred payment plan
3. Its fine teachers
4. Its work/study program

In paragraph form, the same information might look like this:

> There were several reasons why I decided to attend Bingston University. First of all, the tuition was reasonable. Second, the university had a deferred payment plan; this represented a great convenience to my parents. Another reason was the fact that Bingston hires only the finest of teachers to teach in its graduate program. *My chief reason,* however, was Bingston's mandatory work/study program in agriculture, my chosen field: the university requires all agriculture students to gain practical experience by working on local farms while they are still going to school; I knew that this would provide invaluable experience and prepare me to better use the skills I had learned in the classroom.

Now Ask Yourself

1. What is "enumeration by *equal* order"?_____

_____

2. How do *ascending* and *descending* order differ?_____

_____

_____

3. How are simple enumerative lists different from formal enumerative paragraphs?_____

_____

_____

_____

_____

_____

_____

EXERCISE 3–5

Analyzing Enumerative Paragraphs (Simple List Form)

Directions: After studying the diagrams below, read each of the following paragraphs carefully, and determine which order it illustrates (equal, ascending, or descending). Then indicate all *enumerators* and *listing signals* which the author has used to structure the paragraph. Finally, construct a *simple list* which represents the structure of the paragraph. The first has been done as an example.

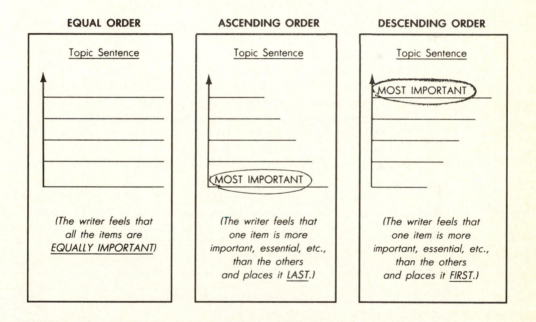

EQUAL ORDER

Topic Sentence

(The writer feels that all the items are EQUALLY IMPORTANT)

ASCENDING ORDER

Topic Sentence

MOST IMPORTANT

(The writer feels that one item is more important, essential, etc., than the others and places it LAST.)

DESCENDING ORDER

Topic Sentence

MOST IMPORTANT

(The writer feels that one item is more important, essential, etc., than the others and places it FIRST.)

Example

1. Of the ten largest cities in the United States in the late 1980s, three are located in the state of Texas. Of these, Houston, which ranks fourth in the country, has the biggest population with 1,705,697 residents. Next comes Dallas, which has 974,243 people and is the seventh largest city in the U.S. The smallest Texas city on the top-ten list is San Antonio, ranking tenth among U.S. cities and having a population of 842,779.

Type of order used: <u>descending order</u>

Enumerator(s): <u>city/population</u>

Listing signals: <u>Next, the smallest (the superlative adjective often acts as</u>
<u>a listing signal)</u>

Paragraph Structure (Simple List Form)

TEXAS CITIES WHICH FIGURE IN THE TOP-TEN LIST

(1.) Houston

2. Dallas

3. San Antonio

2.　　Astronomers use three basic types of telescopes to explore the vastness of space. The *refractor* telescope uses two lenses—one to collect light from a distant object and bring it into focus, and another in the eyepiece to magnify the image. Second, there is the *reflector* telescope, which makes use of a concave mirror instead of a lens to reflect light rays to the upper end of the telescope. Last, and perhaps most important in terms of studying phenomena outside the earth's atmosphere, is the *radio* telescope, which gathers waves with a wire antenna serving as a parabolic reflecting surface. The discovery of mysterious quasars and pulsars was made possible by this kind of telescope.

Type or order used:_____

Enumerator(s):_____

Listing signals:_____

Paragraph Structure (Simple List Form)

_____

_____

_____

_____

3. Air travel, as determined by the number of passengers served in the United States' busiest airports, has been steadily increasing during the latter part of the twentieth century. In 1977, 13.2 million passengers boarded, deplaned, or transferred through Washington, D.C.'s National Airport, while in 1987 that figure rose to over 14.3 million. Next in volume of passengers was San Francisco's International Airport, which served 20.2 million people in 1977 and 28.5 million in 1987. Finally, Chicago's O'Hare Field, the nation's busiest airport both in 1977 and 1987, tallied an increase in air travelers from 44 million to well over 53 million.[2]

Type of order used:_____

Enumerator(s):_____

Listing signals:_____

Paragraph Structure (Simple List Form)

_____

_____

_____

_____

4. Because the earth turns on its axis at the same time as it is moving around the sun, there are two ways to determine the period of time which constitutes a day. It is possible to define a day as the interval of time between the highest point of the sun in the sky on two successive days. This determination, *mean solar time,* produces the twenty-four-hour day when it is averaged out over the year. It is equally possible, however, to define a day as that period of time between the points when the vernal equinox is directly overhead. This method of measuring is called *sidereal time* and is almost four minutes shorter per day than solar mean time.

Type of order used:_____

Enumerator(s):_____

Listing signals:_____

[2] Sources: U.S. Census Bureau and Airport Operators Council International.

Paragraph Structure (Simple List Form)

_____

_____

_____

5.   Educational researchers have identified four distinctive learning styles which students use who are attempting to master new information and concepts. First, some students prefer _auditory_ learning. They learn best from lectures, tape recordings, and class discussions. The second of these styles is _tactile_ learning. This is a learning-by-doing approach, which involves such things as dissecting animals to handle their internal organs rather than reading about them. Still other students are best suited to _experiential_ learning. Making use of all their senses, such as a field trip to a forest when studying botany, is the best way for these learners to understand new material fully. The last of these styles is _visual_ learning. The student who favors this style relies heavily on what can be seen—books and charts, for instance—to acquire knowledge. Of these four learning styles, none is considered best; but rather they are descriptive of techniques individuals use to learn effectively.

Type of order used:_____

Enumerator(s):_____

Listing signals:_____

Paragraph Structure (Simple List Form)

_____

_____

_____

_____

_____

*6.   Bioethicists, a new breed of scientist-philosophers, concern themselves with pressing problems which have arisen as a result of technological advances in modern medicine. One consideration is the recent development of techniques which enable doctors to perform test-tube cross-fertilization, producing the famous test-tube babies. Recombinant DNA, or genetic engineering, is another medical achievement which is accompanied by dubious moral implications. Artificial organ implantation (heart, kidneys, eyes) generates questions of who should be chosen as recipient of these life-sustaining gifts and how these choices should be made. On the opposite end of the spectrum, machines which are capable of prolonging life indefinitely, even though the patient may never regain consciousness, bring up the problem of establishing a precise definition of what death is.

Type of order used:_____

Enumerator(s):_____

Listing signals:_____

Paragraph Structure (Simple List Form)

_____

_____

_____

_____

_____

EXERCISE 3–6

Practicing Ascending and Descending Order

Directions: Working alone, in pairs, or in small groups, study the following paragraph, which probably resembles the paragraph you wrote for Exercise 2–16. On a separate sheet of paper, rewrite the paragraph so that you have arranged the supporting sentences in ascending order (smallest to largest expenditures).

The average elderly household spends over three-fourths of its budget on the necessities of life. The biggest expense is housing, which constitutes 34 percent (over one-third) of the budget. The second largest item is food, representing slightly more than 21 percent, or over one-fifth. Transportation and health care amount to another 25 percent (14.4 and 10.4 percent, respectively), and another 5 percent of the budget is spent on clothing. Thus, these five items alone represent about 80 percent of the budget.

EXERCISE 3–7

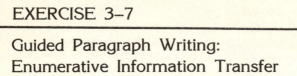

Guided Paragraph Writing:
Enumerative Information Transfer

Directions: Working alone, in pairs, or in small groups, study the following chart. Then, recopy the paragraph that follows on a separate sheet of paper, filling in all the blanks. Some blanks will require only one word; others will require more than one. (Note that the information has been arranged in descending order *by age*, and that it also includes information on the basis of the belief of each of the religions.) As you work, pay attention to the ways the information in the graph has been expressed: You may be able to use some of the same structures and vocabulary in the next writing assignment.

FIVE MAJOR RELIGIONS

	Number of Members	Basis of Belief	Dates of Origin	Geographic Distribution
Judaism	17,981,460	Descent from Israel; *The Torah;* tradition	The exodus of Moses from Egypt (1220 B.C.)	Worldwide
Christianity	1,619,272,560	The teachings of Jesus Christ: *The New Testament*	c. A.D. 33 (Jesus Christ)	Worldwide
Islam	840,221,390	The teachings of Mohammed in *The Koran*	A.D. 570–632 (Mohammed)	Morocco to Indonesia; a large branch in the United States (4,644,000)
Hinduism	647,894,950	*The Vedas* (four books); no common creed	1000 B.C. (?)	India and Eastern countries
Buddhism	307,416,030	The teachings of Buddha in *The Eightfold Way*	563–483 B.C. (Buddha)	The East; spreading to Europe and the United States

The _____ major religions in the world today, which vary according to their ages and bases of belief, are _____ ,

_____ , _____ , _____ , and _____ .
The oldest of these religions is _____ , dating back to
the _____ in _____ B.C. The Jewish faith is
based on _____ , _____ , and _____ .
Next comes Hinduism, which arose around _____ B.C.
Although there is no _____ , the basic beliefs of all
Hindus can be traced back to the four books called _____ .
The third _____ religion, which began between _____
and _____ B.C., is _____ . Its beginnings correspond to the life of _____ , and it is based on his
teachings as found in _____ , its holy book. Fourth, in
terms of age, comes _____ , whose beginnings date
back to the death of _____ in A.D. _____ .
Christ's teachings, as found in the _____ , serve as
the foundation of the Christian belief. And finally,
_____ is the most recently founded of the five religions.
Its origins correspond with the dates of the life of its prophet
_____ ,and its basic creed is based on his teachings as
recorded in _____ .

EXERCISE 3–8

Guided Paragraph Writing: Enumerative Information Transfer

Directions: Using the information in the chart on page 66, write another paragraph, this time arranging the religions in *descending order from the largest to the smallest.*

Phase 1: Exploring Your Topic

Directions: Discuss the assignment with one of your classmates. Should the religions be listed in a different order in the topic sentence? How should they be ordered in the paragraph? What kinds of enumerators and listing signals might be used? (Remember that you will not want to use *the oldest* as was done in Exercise 3–7.)

Phase 2: Writing the First Draft

Directions: Write the first draft of the paragraph. Since your arrangement is based on size, first mention *the size of the religion,* following with information on *geographical distribution.* You may wish to show your paragraph to a different classmate for another opinion on whether the way you have arranged your information clearly demonstrates descending order.

Since you have to repeat the same kind of information several times, try to use some variety in your choice of vocabulary and structures. Note the following.

SIZE

_____ has _____ members (or: adherents, followers).

_____ has a membership of more than _____ .

_____ , with a membership of _____ ,. . . .

NAME

Judaism, the Jewish (or: Hebrew) faith, the Jewish (or: Hebrew) religion
Buddhism, the Buddhist faith, the Buddhist religion
Christianity, the Christian faith, the Christian religion
Islam, the Islamic faith, the Islamic religion
Hinduism, the Hindu faith, the Hindu religion

GEOGRAPHY

_____ is distributed (or: found) worldwide (or: all over the world, in all parts of the world).

_____ , with a worldwide distribution,. . . .

_____ can be found from _____ to _____ .

Phase 3: Making Your Language Accurate

Directions: After you have revised your paragraph based on your classmates' suggestions, you will want to check it for correct usage. First, proofread the sentences to make sure the **subjects** and **verbs** agree. Another common error that learners of English make is **singular-plural** agreement. Notice the examples of this kind of mistake in the following sentences.

> **kinds**
> There are three basic ~~kind~~ of materials that can be found in any good library.

In this sentence, the noun _kind_ must be plural because it is modified by the adjective _three_. The correct form is **kinds.**

resources

One of the most important ~~resource~~ in the library is the reference room.

In this sentence, the noun *resource* must be plural because it is only "one of the . . ." among several other possibilities. The correct form is **resources.**

Now proofread your sentences again to make sure that you have used the correct **subject-verb agreement,** as well as the correct **singular-plural** forms of nouns. After you have corrected any errors, recopy this draft of your paragraph and submit it to your teacher.

EXERCISE 3–9

Paragraph Writing: Enumeration

Phase 1: Exploring Your Topic

Directions: Choose one of the following topics and formulate questions about it. Select key words and phrases from your list of answers and write a topic sentence. If you are working with a partner or in groups, show your topic sentence to your classmates to see if you have limited your topic sufficiently for one paragraph.

General Topics

the qualities of a good wife or husband
the things (at least three) I have learned about Americans since coming to the United States
my favorite kinds of movies

Essay Questions

What type of undergraduate degrees are offered at a particular college or university?
Discuss the advantages of being able to use a computer.
What are the most difficult aspects of learning the English language?

Phase 2: Writing the First Draft

Directions: Using the topic sentence you wrote in Phase 1, write the first draft of a paragraph in which you use *enumeration* to organize your support. Use good examples, details, and so forth in developing your paragraph. Indicate whether you have used ascending, descending, or equal order. When you have finished, you may want to show your paragraph to a classmate to see if it develops your topic sentence clearly.

Phase 3: Making Your Language Accurate

Directions: After you have revised your paragraph based on your classmate's suggestions, you will want to check it for correct usage. Proofread the paragraph to make sure the **subjects** and **verbs** agree. Read through it again to make sure that the **singular** and **plural** forms agree. After you have corrected any errors, recopy this draft and submit it to your teacher.

4

TYPES OF ENUMERATION

Process and Chronology

In this unit we will deal with two specialized types of enumerative paragraphs: the *process* paragraph and the *chronological* (or narrative) paragraph. Since a process paragraph uses many of the listing signals you learned in the previous chapter, we will start with this type.

Process

When supporting sentences are arranged in a step-by-step sequence which *tells how something is made or done*, this development is called *process*. Process development is, in fact, a kind of enumeration, but here we are usually dealing only with *steps* or *stages* (and not, for example, with kinds or types). If we wanted to give a more visual representation of process development, our diagram might look something like this:

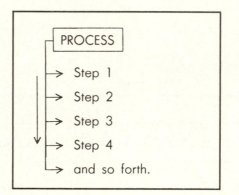

Model Paragraph

In his will, Alfred Nobel left specific instructions as to how the winners of the science awards he endowed are to be selected. First, each year the Swedish Academy of Sciences (physics and chemistry) and the Caroline Medical Institute (physiology and medicine) solicit nearly 2,000 recommendations from past laureates, university professors, and other experts from all over the world. The second step is the review of recommendations received and the selections of preliminary candidates by special committees within the two Swedish institutions. The committee members are specifically instructed that those chosen "shall have conferred the greatest benefit on mankind," and that no consideration be given to the candidates' nationalities. Next, after lengthy investigation and discussion, the final choices are made for each discipline. Finally, telegrams informing them of their awards are sent to the new Nobel laureates about one month prior to the award ceremony.

Now Ask Yourself

1. What are the key words in the topic sentence? (Is there anything in the topic sentence which suggests that the paragraph will be explaining a *process?*)

_____

_____

2. Can you find any enumerative *listing signals?* _____

3. Have any *enumerators* been used (that is, words like *steps* or *stages*)?

_____

_____

_____

EXERCISE 4–1

Analyzing a Process Paragraph (List Form)

Directions: Show the organization of the model paragraph above by filling in the list that follows: You do not have to write complete sentences.

How Nobel Science Laureates _____

1. Two Thousand Requests for _____

2. _____

    a. _____

    b. _____

3. The Final Selection

    a. _____

    b. _____

4. _____

ENUMERATORS

Process paragraphs, like other kinds of enumerative paragraphs, often use enumerators. The difference is that, whereas enumerative paragraphs use many different enumerators (*types, kinds, groups,* and so forth), process paragraphs most commonly use only *three:*

step
stage
phase

Now Ask Yourself

1. Which of these enumerators appear in the paragraphs on finding a suitable apartment (page 13) and changing a flat tire (page 18)? _____

2. What about the model paragraph you just read (the Nobel Prize)?

   _____

3. What is the difference between a *step*, a *stage*, and a *phase*? _____

LISTING SIGNALS

Process paragraphs often use listing signals. *Group 1* listing signals from the previous chapter (page 52) can be used, but the structures which follow them are usually different:

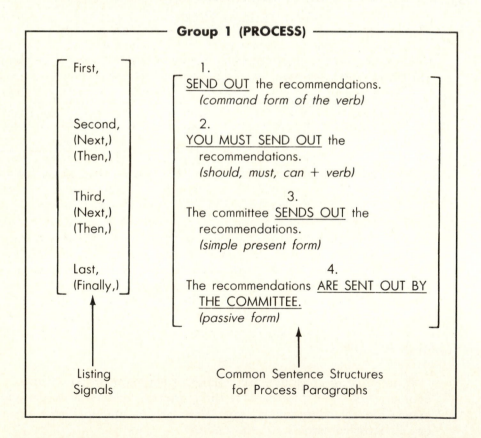

Group 1 (PROCESS)

Listing Signals	Common Sentence Structures for Process Paragraphs
First,	1. <u>SEND OUT</u> the recommendations. *(command form of the verb)*
Second, (Next,) (Then,)	2. <u>YOU MUST SEND OUT</u> the recommendations. *(should, must, can + verb)*
Third, (Next,) (Then,)	3. The committee <u>SENDS OUT</u> the recommendations. *(simple present form)*
Last, (Finally,)	4. The recommendations <u>ARE SENT OUT BY THE COMMITTEE.</u> *(passive form)*

Group 2 listing signals from the previous chapter (page 53) can also be used to develop process paragraphs:

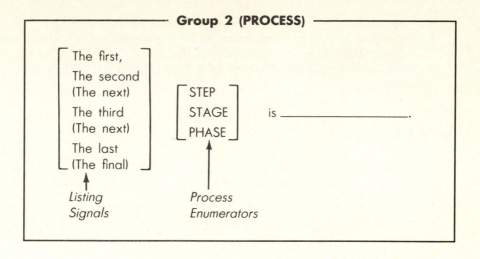

Now Ask Yourself

The following paragraph, from Unit 1, is a paragraph of instruction (a how-to paragraph). Can you make it sound more objective and academic? Working alone, in pairs, or in small groups, rewrite the paragraph on a separate sheet of paper, *avoiding all command forms of verbs*—in other words, make sure that all verbs have subjects, and put them in the passive form. In addition, avoid the word *you*. Finally, be sure to include one or two *listing signals* (if you choose Group 2, use the word *step*) for practice.

> Changing a flat tire is really a very simple operation if you have the right tools. When you have removed the hubcap from the wheel which has the flat, correctly place the jack to lift the car off the ground. Now you are ready to jack up the car high enough for the tire to clear the ground. After you have done that, carefully loosen the nuts that hold the tire and rim in place; the tool you use to do that is called a *lug wrench*. Remove the tire and put the spare tire in place. Now you are ready to put the nuts back on the wheel and tighten them as firmly as you can with the lug wrench. All that remains is to replace the hubcap, lower the car to the ground, give the nuts a final tightening, and remove the jack.

Time Clues, Repetition, and Pronoun Reference

In addition to sequence signals, there are other indicators which a writer can use to develop a process paragraph. They are:

1. *Time clues,* which include choice of verb and tense
2. *Repetition,* which provides links between your sentences, thus helping the reader following your train of thought
3. *Pronoun reference,* which provides still another kind of link between your sentences

TIME CLUES

Study the following model paragraph. It illustrates *time clues.* Later in this chapter it is used to illustrate repetition and pronoun reference.

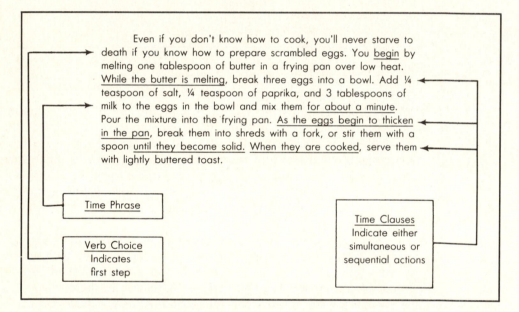

Verb Choice   In the model paragraph, the choice of the verb *begin* indicates the first step or stage. Another appropriate verb choice would be *start.* There are other verbs which can be used to indicate the various parts of a process. Some of them are:

STEP (STAGE)	VERBS
First ⟶	BEGIN START
Intermediate ⟶	CONTINUE BECOME DEVELOP

STEP (STAGE)	VERBS
Final ⟶	END FINISH REMAIN CULMINATE

Time Clauses   Time clauses and phrases also help show the continuity of development in a process. In the model paragraph, the time clauses explain the time relationship between events just as clearly as sequence signals do

While the butter is melting
As the eggs begin to thicken in the pan
When they are cooked

The most common time words used to introduce time clauses are *before, after, when, while, as,* and *until.* Study the following box.

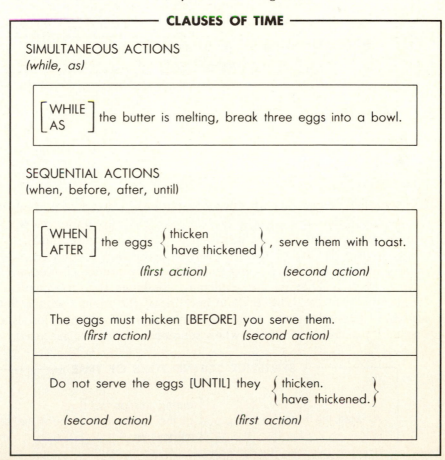

CLAUSES OF TIME

SIMULTANEOUS ACTIONS
(while, as)

[WHILE / AS] the butter is melting, break three eggs into a bowl.

SEQUENTIAL ACTIONS
(when, before, after, until)

[WHEN / AFTER] the eggs {thicken / have thickened}, serve them with toast.
(first action)   *(second action)*

The eggs must thicken [BEFORE] you serve them.
(first action)   *(second action)*

Do not serve the eggs [UNTIL] they {thicken. / have thickened.}

(second action)   *(first action)*

Participial Phrases   Sometimes time clauses may be reduced to *participial phrases*. Study the following box; note that the structure of the clauses is not the same as the structure of the (participial) time phrases.

PARTICIPIAL PHRASES

SIMULTANEOUS ACTIONS
(while)

    Clause: While you are melting the butter, break three eggs into a bowl.

→ Phrase: While melting the butter, . . .

SEQUENTIAL ACTIONS
(when, after, before)

    Clause: [When / After] you have beaten the eggs, pour them into the pan.

→ Phrase: Having beaten the eggs, . . .
             After having beaten the eggs, . . .

    Clause: You must beat the eggs before you pour them into the pan.

→ Phrase: . . . before pouring them into the pan.

Sentence Connectors of Time   Sometimes, instead of making one of the sentences into a time clause, we can join the two sentences by a sentence connector of time. This can be either a word or a phrase. Study the following box. Notice the use of the *semicolon*. A semicolon is used to punctuate the two sentences which are being joined by the sentence connectors in each of the examples. That is, the semicolon combines two grammatically distinct sentences into one. This is done because of the *strong meaning link* between them, expressed by the sentence connectors. The semicolon is commonly used to punctuate sentences when sentence connectors are used.

SENTENCE CONNECTORS OF TIME

A. Melt the butter in the pan; [during this period / at the same time / meanwhile], beat the eggs.

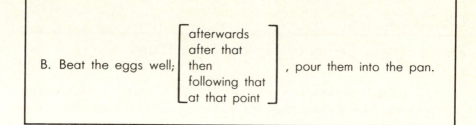

B. Beat the eggs well; [afterwards / after that / then / following that / at that point] , pour them into the pan.

Now Ask Yourself

Can sentences A and B in the preceding box be rewritten using a period in place of the semicolon? If so, rewrite them.

_____

_____

_____

_____

EXERCISE 4-2

Supplying Time Clues

Directions: The following process paragraph is from Unit 1. Notice, however, that all time clues have been removed. Working alone, in pairs, or in small groups, rewrite the paragraph on a separate sheet of paper, adding a few time clues to make it read more smoothly. (Do *not* refer back to Unit 1.) Remember the four kinds of time clues:

1. Verb choice which indicates process
2. Time clause
3. Participial phrase of time
4. Sentence connector of time

In order to find a suitable apartment, you must follow a very systematic approach. You must decide which neighborhood would be most convenient for you. You must determine how much rent your budget will allow. You must check the classified ads in the newspapers. Be sure to check these ads regularly, since new listings appear each day. Telephone the apartments which seem likely choices. Begin your long journey to inspect each one of them.

EXERCISE 4–3

Paraphrasing Sentences Using Time Clues

Directions: The following sentences are based on the model paragraph dealing with the Nobel Prize (page 72). Rewrite each of the sentences in two different ways, using the words or phrases indicated. Pay attention to *punctuation*. In the case of participial phrases, make sure that the subject of the sentence is the same as the implied subject of the participial phrase.

1. The Swedish Academy of Science solicits recommendations in the fields of physics and chemistry; the Caroline Medical Institute solicits recommendations in the fields of physiology and medicine.

   (while) While the Swedish Academy of Science solicits recommendations in the fields of physics and chemistry, the Caroline Medical Institute solicits recommendations in the fields of physiology and medicine.

   (at the same time) The Swedish Academy of Science _____

   _____

   _____

2. Requests are sent out; recommendations are received from past laureates, university professors, and experts all over the world.

   (after) _____

   _____

   (after that) _____

   _____

3. The committees receive all recommendations; they begin reviewing them.

   (when) _____

   _____

   (PARTICIPIAL PHRASE)   Having _____

   _____

4. The committee members review the recommendations; they are instructed that no consideration be given to the candidates' nationalities.

   (as) _____

   _____

   (at the same time) _____

5. The committee members review the recommendations; preliminary choices are made.

(PARTICIPIAL PHRASE) ___Having___

_____

(before) _____

_____

6. The committees conduct lengthy investigations and have long discussions; the final choices are made.

(PARTICIPIAL PHRASE) ___After having___

_____

(until) _____

_____

7. The final choices are made; telegrams are sent to the new Nobel laureates.

(PARTICIPIAL PHRASE) _After making_

_____

(then) _____

_____

(until) _____

_____

(VERB CHOICE—final step) _____

_____

REPETITION AND PRONOUN REFERENCE

Words are often repeated to add continuity to a paragraph. They are repeated either in their *original* form or in *pronoun* form. In the following model paragraph, note:

the words *eggs, bowl,* and *mix* (as well as its word form *mixture*);
the different pronouns which mean *egg.*

These things, in addition to sequence signals, add continuity and *cohesiveness* to a paragraph's development, and are particularly important in a process paragraph. Pay attention to this sort of clue when you write.

Model Paragraph

Even if you don't know how to cook, you'll never starve to death if you know how to prepare scrambled eggs. You begin by melting one tablespoon of butter in a frying pan over low heat. While the butter is melting, break three eggs into a bowl. Add ¼ teaspoon of salt, ¼ teaspoon of paprika, and 3 tablespoons of milk to the eggs in the bowl and mix them for about a minute. Pour the mixture into the frying pan. As the eggs begin to thicken in the pan, break them into shreds with a fork, or stir them with a spoon until they become solid. When they are cooked, serve them with lightly buttered toast.

EXERCISE 4–4

Unscrambling a Process Paragraph

Directions: The following two groups of sentences constitute paragraphs on the processes known as the scientific method and culture shock. However, the sentences have been given a *disordered sequence*—that is, they have been *scrambled.* Place them in their correct order and then recopy the reconstructed paragraphs, double-spaced, onto a separate sheet of paper. Circle all repeated words and draw lines to connect them. Underline all pronoun forms and draw arrows to the words they represent.

The Scientific Method

1. Following this method, the researcher first observes some aspects of nature and then poses a specific question about what has been observed.
2. Experiments based on this hypothesis are designed and conducted to test each contingency.
3. In order to answer this question, pertinent data are collected.
4. After thorough experimentation, the researcher validates, modifies, or rejects the original hypothesis.
5. Originating from the branch of philosophy called epistemology, what we now know as the scientific method provides guidelines for the systematic acquisition of knowledge.
6. On the basis of these data, a hypothesis is proposed to explain them.

Culture Shock

1. The visitor has usually learned the language and is thus able to laugh at himself or herself.
2. Having passed through these stages of culture shock, the visitor may even eventually return home with regret at having lost his or her adopted home.
3. The process of reacting and adjusting to a new society, sometimes termed *culture shock,* has four distinct stages.
4. A hostile attitude is typical of the second stage, which develops at that point when the individual has to cope seriously with the day-to-day problems of housing, shopping, transportation, and so forth.
5. Final adjustment to a new culture occurs when the visitor is able to function without anxiety and to accept what he or she finds for what it is—another way of doing things.
6. During these initial encounters, every aspect of the new society seems fascinating.
7. The first period, or honeymoon stage, may last as long as several months.
8. The visitor develops a sense of humor about his or her problems on entering the third stage.
9. The visitor usually begins his or her stay in a hotel and meets sympathetic and gracious nationals.
10. The visitor soon finds that most people in the new society are indifferent to these problems, and so seeks out fellow countrymen to support him or her in criticism of the host country.

EXERCISE 4–5

Guided Paragraph Writing: Process Information Transfer

Directions: Working alone, in pairs, or in small groups, study the following series of drawings that represents a process. Then, on a separate sheet of paper, recopy the paragraph, filling in all the blanks. Some blanks will require only one word; others will require more than one. Pay special attention to verbs in parentheses ( )—they must be put in the proper form.

Useful Definitions

butterfly—an adult insect with four wings, often brightly colored
caterpillar—the wormlike form of a butterfly in its first stage of development

The Metamorphosis of a Caterpillar into a Butterfly

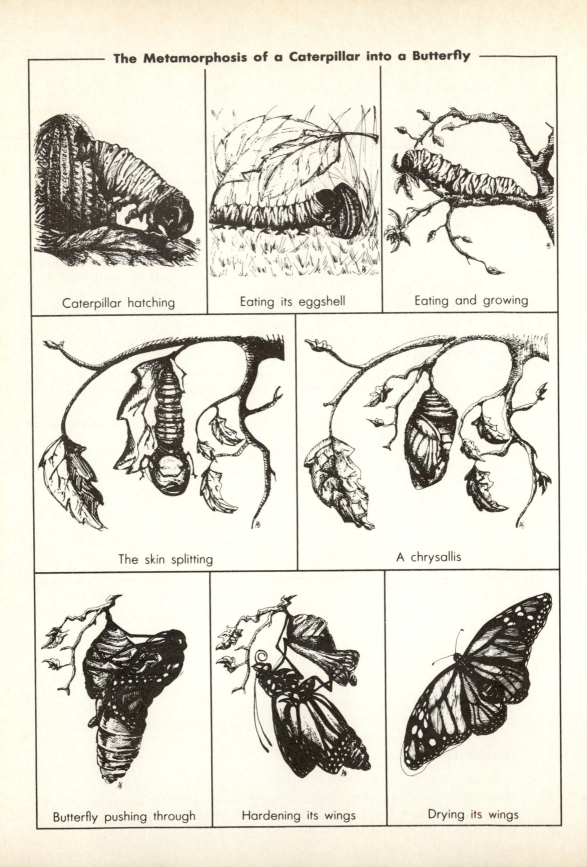

Caterpillar hatching

Eating its eggshell

Eating and growing

The skin splitting

A chrysallis

Butterfly pushing through

Hardening its wings

Drying its wings

pupa—the stage of development which is between the caterpillar and the butterfly

to hatch—to break out of an egg

to split—to break open

chrysallis—the case that covers a pupa

The metamorphosis of a _____ into a _____ is one of the wonders of nature. The _____ step (occur) _____ when the _____ (hatch) _____ from its egg. Next, it (eat) _____ the eggshell from which it (hatch) _____ . After (eat) _____ and (grow) _____ fat, the caterpillar is ready (attach) _____ itself to a leaf, where its skin (begin, split) _____ , revealing the _____ . The pupa (grow, soon) _____ a protective cover called a _____ . _____ this phase, which lasts _____ , the caterpillar (begin, change) _____ , (develop) _____ into a mature insect. In the _____ phase, a young butterfly (push) _____ through the chrysallis and (force) _____ its way free. After (hang) _____ upside down to harden its wings, it then (spread out, them) _____ to dry. It is now ready (fly away) _____ and spend its adult life as one of nature's most beautiful creatures.

EXERCISE 4–6

Paragraph Writing: Process

Phase 1: Exploring Your Topic

Directions: Construct a simple list showing the steps in one or both of the following processes, depending on your teacher's instructions. If you are working with a partner or in groups, compare your list with your classmates' to see if you have included all the steps.

General Topic Sentence

Knowing how to operate a VCR permits you to enjoy watching your favorite movies at home.

Essay Question

Applying to a school in the United States or in (your country) can sometimes be a rather time-consuming process. List and briefly describe the steps in such a process.

Phase 2: Writing the First Draft

Directions: Taking the topic which you have chosen, write the first draft of the paragraph in which you expand the list you prepared in Phase 1 into sentences explaining the process. When you have finished your draft, you may wish to show it to a classmate to see if you have included all the steps in the process.

Phase 3: Making Your Language Accurate

Directions: After you have revised your paragraph based on your classmate's suggestions, you will want to check it for correct usage. Proofread the sentences to make sure that the **subjects** and **verbs** and **singular-plural forms** agree. Another frequent language error involves **tense.** Notice the following examples of this type of mistake.

> **begins** **meets**
> The visitor usually ~~begin~~ his or her stay in a hotel and ~~met~~ sympathetic and gracious nationals.

In this sentence, the adverb *usually* indicates that the actions are habitual; therefore, the present tense is used for *both* verbs (present and past tense usually are not mixed like this). These verbs should be **begins** and **meets.**

> **has learned**
> After a person ~~is learning~~ the language, he or she begins to feel more comfortable.

In this sentence, the time word *after* takes either present or present perfect tense. The verb should be either **learns** or **has learned.**

Proofread the sentences in your paragraph again to make sure that you have used appropriate tenses. After you have corrected any errors, recopy this draft of your paragraph and submit it to your teacher.

Chronological Order

When the order in which things happen, or a *time sequence,* is used to develop a paragraph, this is called *chronological order.* Like process, this is a special form of enumeration, since it is really a *list of events.*

Model Paragraph

> Although the U.S. Air Force was not officially created until after the second World War, it had existed under other names

since the beginning of the century. The Army Air Forces were started on August 1, 1907, as a part of the Aeronautical Division of the U.S. Signal Corps, and it was more than one year later that this small division carried out its first mission in its own airplane. When the United States entered World War I in 1917, the Aviation Service, as it was then called, had only thirty-five pilots. On December 7, 1941, the renamed Army Air Forces had only 3,000 of their 10,000 planes ready for combat. Finally, in 1947, the U.S. Air Force was established as a separate branch of the military.

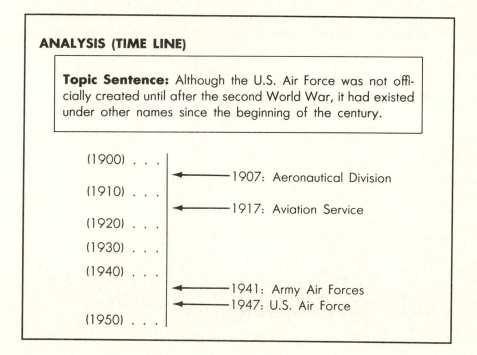

ANALYSIS (TIME LINE)

Topic Sentence: Although the U.S. Air Force was not officially created until after the second World War, it had existed under other names since the beginning of the century.

(1900) . . .

←——————1907: Aeronautical Division

(1910) . . .

←——————1917: Aviation Service

(1920) . . .

(1930) . . .

(1940) . . .

←——————1941: Army Air Forces
←——————1947: U.S. Air Force

(1950) . . .

Now Ask Yourself

1. Why do we classify chronological order as enumeration? _____

_____

2. What are the key words in the topic sentence of the model paragraph?

_____

3. What four main examples are given? _____

_____

4. What statistics have been used? _____

_____

5. Do you notice any enumerators and listing signals? _____

_____

Any time clauses? (Underline them in the paragraph.)

LISTING SIGNALS

Enumerators are rarely used in chronological order. We might occasionally write "the next *thing*" or "the next *event*," but the reader usually does not need this kind of signal to understand what is being discussed.

However, we do often use *Group 1* process listing signals. Refer back to page 74 to refresh your memory.

Now Ask Yourself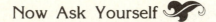

Comparing the forms of the verbs in the box on page 74 with the forms of the verbs in the model paragraph which you have just read, what is one way in which *process* differs from *narrative chronological order?*

_____

_____

_____

_____

_____

_____

TIME CLUES

Time clues of all kinds are, of course, used *very* often in chronology. Once again, however, as with listing signals, the forms of the verbs generally are not present forms, as they were in process, but rather *past* forms. In addition, prepositional phrases of time often appear.

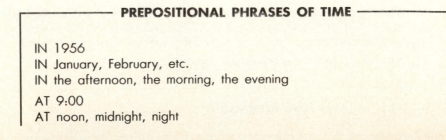

┌─── **PREPOSITIONAL PHRASES OF TIME** ───

IN 1956
IN January, February, etc.
IN the afternoon, the morning, the evening

AT 9:00
AT noon, midnight, night

ON Monday, Tuesday, etc.
ON July 6
ON July 6, 1955

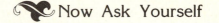 Now Ask Yourself

Which prepositions of time are used with the following:

1. Days of the week? _____

2. Months of the year? _____

3. An exact date? _____

4. Parts of the day? (two prepositions) _____

5. A specific year? _____

6. A particular hour of the day? _____

EXERCISE 4–7

Controlled Writing: Tense Shift

Directions: Rewrite the model process paragraph on page 72 (Nobel Prize winners). This time, assume that the entire process occurred several months ago. In other words, describe it as though you were describing a real past event. The topic sentence has been provided for you.

> Earlier this year, preparations were made once again to pick the new Nobel science laureates.

EXERCISE 4–8

Unscrambling a Chronological Paragraph

Directions: Place the following scrambled sentences in their correct order; use the time line as your work space. Then, if your teacher wishes, copy the reconstructed paragraph on a separate sheet of paper.

1. First, I had to return some overdue books to the library.
2. After my early class, I had a quick cup of coffee with some friends in the cafeteria.
3. I got up at 6:30 A.M. as usual.

4. I went to my accounting class.
5. The subway train was a little late, so I arrived just in time for my 8:30 class.
6. I left my apartment at 7:45.
7. Before my next class, I had several things to do.
8. I also had to see my advisor in his office at 10:45 to review my schedule for next semester.
9. Yesterday morning was typical of my busy life as a student.
10. After having planned my schedule, I had just enough time to review my notes before my 11:30 accounting class.
11. By 1:00 I was ready for a big lunch to help get me through the rest of my day.

ANALYSIS (Time Line)

Topic Sentence:

```
(6:00 A.M.) . . . .
(7:00 A.M.) . . . .
(8:00 A.M.) . . . .
(9:00 A.M.) . . . .
(10:00 A.M.) . . . .
(11:00 A.M.) . . . .
(12:00 P.M.) . . . .
(1:00 P.M.) . . . .
```

EXERCISE 4–9

Unscrambling a Chronological Paragraph

Directions: The following sentences constitute a paragraph about Abraham Lincoln (February 12, 1809–April 14, 1865), the sixteenth president of the United States. Unscramble them by placing them in their correct order; use the time line as your work space. Then, if your teacher wishes, copy the reconstructed paragraph on a separate sheet of paper.

1. After having served only this one term in the U.S. Congress, he was defeated for reelection and returned to practice law in Springfield.
2. It was there that, having first tried his hand at a variety of occupations (storekeeper, postmaster, surveyor), he first became interested in politics.
3. He won the election, thus becoming the sixteenth president of the United States.
4. However, he was successful in his subsequent attempts, and served four two-year terms in the state legislature, from 1834 to 1842.
5. Shortly after becoming a lawyer, he moved to Springfield, Illinois to set up his own law office.
6. Lincoln's early political career did not foreshadow the success he was to have in politics.
7. Indeed, he had almost entirely lost any hope of holding political office when, in 1854, the slavery question once again forced him into the political arena.
8. He was not successful the first time he ran for office in 1831.
9. During this same period, he added the study of law to his legislative duties, finally completing his legal studies in 1836.
10. In 1846, he was elected to the United States House of Representatives for two years.
11. Although he was defeated twice for election to the U.S. Congress, he finally managed, in 1860, to be nominated by the Republican Party as its candidate for president.
12. In his early twenties he moved to Illinois.

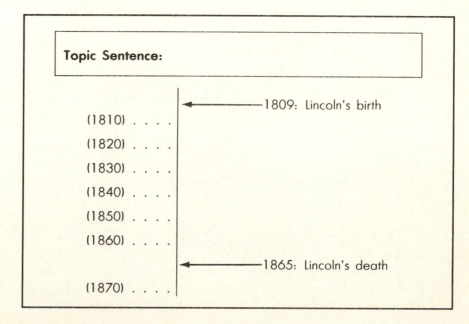

EXERCISE 4–10

Guided Paragraph Writing:
Chronological Information Transfer

Directions: Working alone, in pairs, or in small groups, study the following time line. Then, on a separate sheet of paper, recopy the paragraph, filling in all the blanks. Some blanks will require only one word; others will require more than one. Pay special attention to verbs in parentheses ( )—they must be put in the proper form.

Before you begin, familiarize yourself with the meaning of the following terms:

to culminate	cum laude
the Army	term
the Navy	the Marine Corps
an overwhelming majority	an incumbent

(1940)——— ◄— 1940: Graduated cum laude from Harvard; published *Why England Slept*

◄—1945: Awarded Navy and U.S. Marine Corps medal for heroism in combat

◄—1946: Elected to the U.S. House of Representatives from Massachusetts by an overwhelming majority (two-year term)

(1950)——— 1948–51: Served second and third terms as a member of Congress; won second and third elections by an even greater majority than the first

◄—1952: Defeated incumbent Henry Cabot Lodge for a seat in the U.S. Senate

◄—1958: Reelected to the Senate by the largest majority in Massachusetts history

(1960)———|◄—1960: Narrowly defeated Richard Nixon to be-
come the first Roman Catholic President of
the United States

John F. Kennedy's early career (give) <u>gave</u> a clear indication
of his later political success, which would culminate in his eventual
election to the Presidency of the United States. As an undergraduate at Harvard University, he (achieve) _____ consid-
erable academic distinction and (graduate) _____ cum laude
in _____, the same year that his first book, *Why England
Slept,* (publish) _____. Soon after that, he joined the military
and (become) _____ well known for his bravery: In _____,
he (win) _____ both the Navy and Marine Corps medals for
_____. _____ year later, he (add) _____ politics to his
already impressive list of achievements when he (elect)
_____ to Congress by an overwhelming majority of the people
of _____, his home state. His popularity (continue, grow)
_____, and by the time he was thirty-three, he (won)
_____ a total of three elections to Congress, the last two by
an even greater majority than the first. His tenure in the House
of Representatives (follow, soon) _____ by the start of an
equally impressive career in the Senate, when he (defeat)
_____ incumbent Henry Cabot Lodge in _____ for the position of Senator from Massachusetts—a success which Kennedy
was to repeat _____ years later, when the voters (reelect)
_____ him by the largest majority in that state's history. The
final triumph (occur) _____ in _____, when he narrowly (defeat)
_____ Richard Nixon, (become) _____ the first Roman Catholic president of the United States.

EXERCISE 4–11

Paragraph Writing: Chronology

Phase 1: Exploring Your Topic

Directions: Select one of the following topics and prepare a time line to note
the achievements events in that person's life which you may want to include.
After studying the time line carefully, select those events which have made
that person successful or important. Then, write a topic sentence indicating
that your paragraph will discuss the events which contributed to his or her

success. If you are working with a partner or in groups, you may wish to show your topic sentence and time line to your classmates to see if the chronology supports your topic sentence.

General Topic

the most successful person in your family

Essay Question

Discuss the events in the life of (a leader in your country) which contributed to his or her success.

Note: If you choose the academic topic, you may wish to use information from Exercise 1–2.

Phase 2: Writing the First Draft

Directions: Write the first draft of a chronological paragraph in which you use the information on your time line. When you have finished, you may wish to show your paragraph to a classmate to see if the chronology is complete.

Phase 3: Making Your Language Accurate

Directions: After you have revised your paragraph based on your classmate's suggestions, you will want to check it for correct usage. Proofread the paragraph to make sure that the **subjects** and **verbs** and **singular-plural forms** agree and that you have used the appropriate **tenses.** After you have corrected any errors, recopy this draft of your paragraph and submit it to your teacher.

5

CAUSE AND EFFECT

In Unit 3, you learned how to divide a topic into its various types, characteristics, elements, parts, and so forth. Now we will concentrate on a type of paragraph development which frequently is similar to enumeration: *cause and effect.* In other words, when you use a cause-effect method of development, this will often mean that you are supporting your topic sentence by listing or enumerating.

Remember, however, that in a cause-effect development, there is always a *causal relationship* between the topic sentence and the supporting sentences, or even between major supporting sentences and minor ones. This means that your supporting sentences become a list of either *effects* (what a certain situation has led to or has resulted in), or *causes* (reasons or explanations why something is the way it is, or why it happened the way it did).

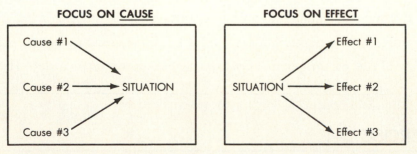

We will look at each of these methods in the model paragraphs which follow. As you study each of them, look for: 1) supportive material such as examples, details, anecdotes, facts and statistics; 2) listing signals (enumeration); 3) ascending vs. descending order.

Cause-Effect Development: Focus on *Effect*

Model Paragraph

Some scientists warn that the gradual warming of the earth's atmosphere, known as the Greenhouse Effect, will cause dramatic changes in the world as we now know it. First of all, because of the increase in temperature of up to 10 degrees F by the end of the next century, which some believe has already begun, there will be changes in existing patterns of agriculture. Such fertile areas as the U.S. Great Plains may become deserts, while the now arid lands in Saudi Arabia may become grain-producing farmland. Secondly, since rainfall patterns will change, water supplies in some areas will diminish. Experts predict, for instance, that the rice fields in southeast Asia will someday require irrigation to sustain crops. Changes in water levels will also be responsible for altered living patterns. Coastal areas, such as Florida and the Netherlands, will experience such a dramatic rise in water levels that they will fall below sea level and become uninhabitable. In other areas, like the Great Lakes, water levels will fall; consequently, they will no longer be able to support industry with energy supplies and a ready means of transportation. Since most experts on the Greenhouse Effect are convinced that it is irreversible, they advise us to plan now for how best to cope with a changing world.

Notice that the topic sentence introduces the idea of cause (that is, the Greenhouse Effect) and effect (that is, what it will do to change the world as we now know it). The supporting sentences list (enumerate) and *explain* these effects.

Now Ask Yourself ❧

1. Have any enumerative listing signals been used?_____

_____

2. Is the paragraph in *ascending, descending,* or *equal* order? How can you tell?_____

EXERCISE 5–1

Analyzing a Cause-Effect Paragraph (Focus on Effect)

Directions: Fill in the following chart, which is based on the preceding model paragraph.

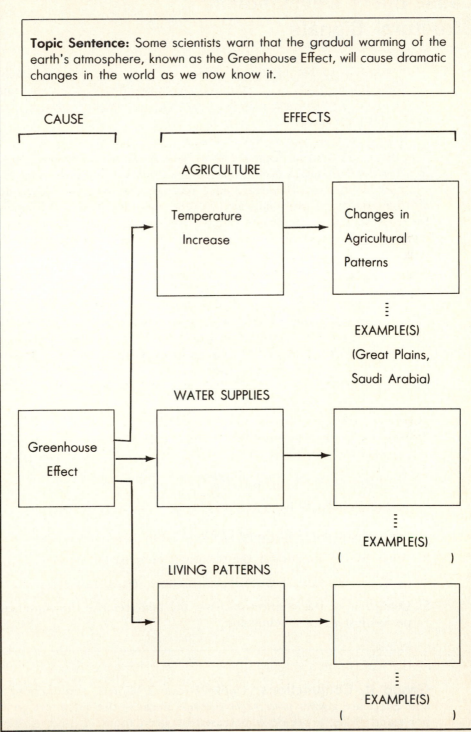

Topic Sentence: Some scientists warn that the gradual warming of the earth's atmosphere, known as the Greenhouse Effect, will cause dramatic changes in the world as we now know it.

CAUSE

EFFECTS

AGRICULTURE

Temperature Increase

Changes in Agricultural Patterns

EXAMPLE(S)
(Great Plains, Saudi Arabia)

WATER SUPPLIES

Greenhouse Effect

EXAMPLE(S)
(   )

LIVING PATTERNS

EXAMPLE(S)
(   )

Cause-Effect Development: Structural Signals

In addition to listing signals (First . . . , Second . . . , Finally, . . . ; the first cause-effect . . . , the second cause-effect . . . , the final cause-effect . . .), certain other basic structures are used commonly in writing cause-effect paragraphs.

Group I. Sentence Connectors. These are words and phrases used to join *two complete grammatical sentences.* A semicolon (;) is often used before a sentence connector. However, since each of the sentences can stand alone and be considered grammatically correct, a period (.) can also be used after the first sentence. In either case, a comma (,) is used *after* the sentence connector.

A.

In some areas, water levels will fall;	**as a result, consequently, therefore, because of this, hence,**	these areas will no longer be able to support industry.
(Cause)		(Effect)

Now Ask Yourself

1. Which sentence is this kind of connector attached to—the one expressing *cause* or the one expressing *effect*?_____

2. What are the names for the following punctuation marks?

   (.)_____ (,)_____ (;)_____

3. Using one of the connectors from the box, rewrite the sentences with a period instead of a semicolon.

   _____

Group II. Conjunctions. Unlike Group 1 signals, conjunctions of cause and effect are always *preceded by commas.* Because the sentences generally do not stand alone, a period is not used between them.

A.

In some areas, water levels   [**so**]   these areas will no longer

                  will fall,   be able to support industry.

     (   )   (   )

B.

Some areas will no longer   [**for**]   water levels will have fallen

be able to support industry,   in these areas.

     (   )   (   )

Now Ask Yourself

1. Which parts of the preceding sentences express cause? Effect? (Fill in the parentheses.)
2. In which sentence does the order of the cause and the effect resemble the order of Group 1? How does the punctuation differ?
3. Rewrite sentence B using *therefore*. Be sure to punctuate correctly.

In some areas, _____

_____

Group III. Clause Structures. Box A of this group consists of signals whose parts are separated: *so . . . that, such . . . that,* and *such a . . . that.*

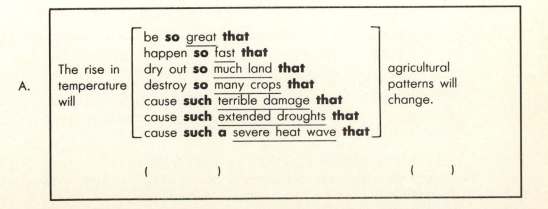

A.

The rise in temperature will

- be **so** great **that**
- happen **so** fast **that**
- dry out **so** much land **that**
- destroy **so** many crops **that**
- cause **such** terrible damage **that**
- cause **such** extended droughts **that**
- cause **such a** severe heat wave **that**

agricultural patterns will change.

     (   )   (   )

Now Ask Yourself

1. Which sentences express cause? Effect? (Fill in the parentheses.)
2. Show that you understand the difference in usage between *so . . . that,* *such . . . that,* and *such a/an . . . that* by filling in the blanks. After you have finished, try to state a rule for using these structures.

> There will be _____ great rise in temperature that agricultural patterns will change. This change will occur _____ suddenly and farmers will be _____ unprepared for it that agriculture may even die out in some sections of the United States. In fact, _____ many farmers will be ruined that fewer people may want to become farmers in the future. But even if the number of farmers does not diminish, the great shift in agriculture will have _____ unpleasant consequences that no one will be unaffected by it. It will cause _____ acute hardship and _____ much unhappiness all over the United States that the people may well remember it for centuries.

3. Take one of the sentences in box A and rewrite it using *consequently.* Be sure to punctuate correctly.

   There will be a _____

   _____ .

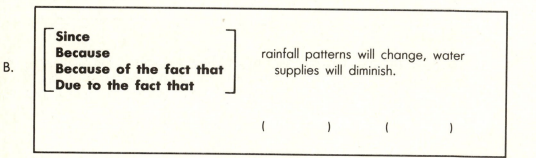

B.

| Since
 Because
 Because of the fact that
 Due to the fact that | rainfall patterns will change, water supplies will diminish. |

(   )   (   )

Now Ask Yourself

1. Which sentence expresses cause? Effect? (Fill in the parentheses.)
2. Using the word *because,* rewrite the sentences, reversing the order of the cause and the effect. Note that you will not need a comma.

_____

3. Now rewrite the sentence using *because of this.* Be sure to punctuate correctly.

_____

Group IV. Phrase Structures. Because a phrase (a group of words) is not a complete sentence, it *must* be connected to the main sentence.

Because of
Due to
As a result of
In view of
the increased heat, agricultural patterns will change.

(   )   (   )

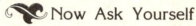 Now Ask Yourself

1. Which part of the sentence expresses cause? Effect? (Fill in the parentheses.)
2. Rewrite the sentence in the box above with *due to*, reversing the order of the parts. Note that you will not need a comma.

_____

3. Now write the same sentence with *because* (not *because of*).

_____

4. Now write the same sentence with *as a result* (not *as a result of*).

_____

Group V. Predicate Structures. The predicate of a sentence includes everything from the verb to the end. In this group of structures, the cause-effect relationship is indicated either by the verb or the words following it.

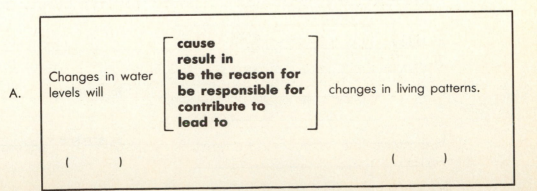

A.   Changes in water levels will

cause
result in
be the reason for
be responsible for
contribute to
lead to

changes in living patterns.

(   )   (   )

Now Ask Yourself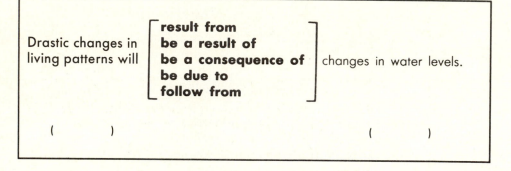

1. Which part of the sentence expresses cause? Effect? (Fill in the parentheses.)
2. Remembering that the verb *to cause* is sometimes followed by an *object* plus an *infinitive* (the *to-* form of a verb), complete the following:

_____ will cause _____

to _____ .

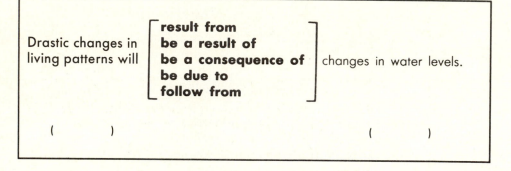

B.   Drastic changes in living patterns will
$$\begin{bmatrix} \text{result from} \\ \text{be a result of} \\ \text{be a consequence of} \\ \text{be due to} \\ \text{follow from} \end{bmatrix}$$
changes in water levels.

(   )   (   )

Now Ask Yourself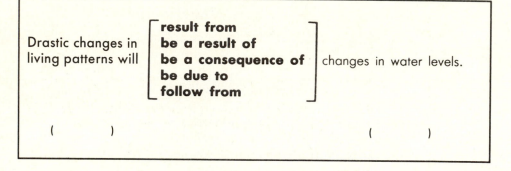

1. Which part of the sentence expresses cause? Effect? (Fill in the parentheses.)
2. On a separate sheet of paper, rewrite sentence B in each of the following ways, identifying the cause and the effect in each sentence. Be sure to punctuate properly.

a. _____ will result in _____

_____ .

b. Due to the fact that _____

_____ .

c. _____ As a result, _____

_____ .

d. Due to _____

_____ .

e. _____ consequently _____

_____ .

f. _____ as a result of _____

_____ .

Group VI. Participial Phrases. Notice that the participial phrases in the following box (1) have no subjects, and (2) contain verbs which are in the -*ing* form. Since a participial phrase has no subject, it *must* be connected to the main sentence. Some of the structures in Group 4 can be used to create such phrases.

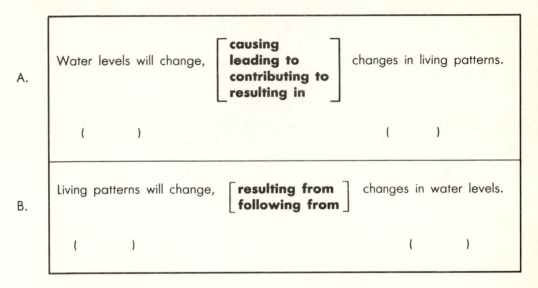

A.

Water levels will change,   ⎡ **causing**
                            leading to   changes in living patterns.
                            contributing to
                            resulting in ⎦

(   )   (   )

B.

Living patterns will change,   ⎡ **resulting from**
                               following from ⎦   changes in water levels.

(   )   (   )

Now Ask Yourself

1. Which parts of the sentences express cause? Effect? (Fill in the parentheses.)
2. Remembering the other structure of the verb *to cause*, complete the following:

_____ , causing _____

to_____ .

EXERCISE 5–2

Paraphrasing Sentences of Cause-Effect

Directions: The following sentences are based on the model paragraph on page 96.

1. Rewrite each of the sentences in **two** different ways, using the words and phrases which have been indicated.
2. Pay particular attention to punctuation.
3. Indicate the **cause** and the **effect** in the parentheses beneath each sentence, as in the example.

Example:

1. Since most experts are convinced that the Greenhouse Effect is irreversible, they advise us to plan now for how best to cope with a changing world.

   (therefore) <u>Most experts are convinced that the</u>

   <u>Greenhouse Effect is irreversible;</u>
   (cause)

   <u>therefore, they advise us to plan now</u>
   (effect)

   <u>for how best to cope with a changing world.</u>

   (due to) <u>Due to most experts' conviction that the</u>

   <u>Greenhouse Effect is irreversible, they</u>
   (cause)

   <u>advise us to plan now for how best to</u>
   (effect)

   <u>cope with a changing world.</u>

2. Massive shifts in population will result from all of these environmental changes.

   (hence)_____

   _____

   (because of)_____

   _____

3. The Greenhouse Effect will cause dramatic changes in the way we live.

   (resulting from)_____

   _____

   (will follow from)_____

   _____

4. Other areas will experience a fall in water levels; consequently, they will no longer be able to support industry.

   (will result in)_____

   _____

   (because)_____

   _____

5. Because of the increase in temperature, existing patterns of agriculture will change.

(so/such . . . that)_____

_____

(since)_____

_____

6. Because rainfall patterns will change, water supplies in some areas will diminish.

(hence)_____

_____

(due to)_____

_____

EXERCISE 5-3

Guided Paragraph Writing:
Cause-Effect Information Transfer

Directions: Working alone, in pairs, or in small groups, study the cause-effect chart. Then, on a separate sheet of paper, recopy the paragraph, filling in all the blanks. Some blanks will require only one word; others will require more than one. Before you begin, familiarize yourself with the meanings of the words in the chart.

VITAMIN	RESULT(S) OF DEFICIENCY
A	Night blindness; skin infection; degeneration of mucous membranes
B_1	Beriberi; nervous disorders
B_6 and B_{12}	Pernicious anemia; poor metabolism
C	Scurvy
D	Rickets
K	Hemorrhaging

A lack of essential vitamins—that is, those vitamins which are necessary for health and normal body function—can result _____ serious illness. Vitamin A, for example, helps prevent the _____ from (become) _____ infected. A lack _____ this vitamin can lead _____ night blindness or (cause, even, can) _____ mucous membranes (degenerate) _____. A second essential vitamin (be) _____ vitamin B_1. People who (have, not) _____ enough B_1 sometimes contract a disease called _____ and can be troubled by various _____. Serious problems (create, can, also) _____ by an inadequate supply of the vitamins B_6 and B_{12}. When the body (lack) _____ the _____ amount of B_6 and B_{12}, _____ and _____ (result, can) _____. Two other important vitamins are vitamin C and vitamin D. The disease scurvy (result, can) _____ a deficiency of vitamin C, while a diet that is deficient in vitamin D (lead, can) _____ a condition known as rickets (a disease which makes bones so soft that they bend). A final—but by no means *the* final—example of a disease or condition that (bring about, can) _____ by a lack of essential vitamins is _____, or uncontrolled bleeding. Such bleeding can occur in people _____ diets (include, not) _____ vitamin K.

EXERCISE 5–4

Paragraph Writing: Cause-Effect (Focus on Effect)

Phase 1: Exploring Your Topic

Directions: Select one of the following topics and write down all the effects—either positive or negative—you can think of. From this list, select the three effects which you consider most significant. Then, write a topic sentence indicating that you will describe these effects. If you are working with a partner or in groups, you may wish to show your topic sentence to your classmates to see if it is appropriate for the effects you plan to write about.

General Topic

the effects a teacher has had on your personality, your feelings about school, or your approach to life in general

Essay Question

What effects has improved technology (in communication, transportation, agriculture, and so forth) had on life in (your country)?

Phase 2: Writing the First Draft

Directions: Write the first draft of a paragraph in which you focus on effects. When you have finished, you may wish to show your paragraph to a classmate to see if you have developed the cause-effect relationship clearly.

Phase 3: Making Your Language Accurate

Directions: After you have revised your paragraph based on your classmate's suggestions, you will want to check it for correct usage. Proofread the paragraph to make sure that the **subjects** and **verbs** and **singular-plural** forms agree and that you have used the appropriate **tenses.**

Another common usage error is inaccurate **pronoun reference.** Notice the examples of this type of error in the following sentences.

> The Greenhouse Effect will cause dramatic changes in the
>
> **it**
> world as we know ~~him.~~

In this sentence, the pronoun refers to an inanimate noun, *world*. The correct form is **it.**

> **they**
> Water levels will fall in the Great Lakes; consequently, ~~it~~
> will no longer be able to support industry.

In this sentence, the pronoun refers to a plural noun, *Great Lakes*. The correct form is **they.**

Proofread your paragraph again to make sure that all pronouns are used accurately. After you have corrected any errors, recopy this draft of your paragraph and submit it to your teacher.

Cause-Effect Development: Focus on *Cause*

Model Paragraph

Why is it that American working women complain about job discrimination? Statistics suggest that there is a basis for their grievances. According to recent Census Bureau statistics, nearly 45 percent of all women of working age are in the labor force. Although they have made progress in recent years, women are still underrepresented in traditionally male professions. For example, women constitute only 9.4 percent of electrical engineers, 17.4 percent of doctors, and 15.2 percent of lawyers. A second area of complaint is women's median weekly and yearly earnings in comparison with men's. The average male factory worker earns $336 per week, while a female worker earns only $225.

Further, the salary gap is even more pronounced among women with higher educations. The average woman college graduate makes $21,889 annually, but the average male college graduate makes $33,934, a difference of 55 percent.

Now Ask Yourself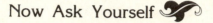

1. Which sentence is the topic sentence—the first, the second, or both taken together?_____

2. Have any enumerative listing signals been used?_____
3. Is the paragraph in equal, ascending, or descending order? How can you tell?_____

EXERCISE 5–5

Analyzing a Cause-Effect Paragraph (Focus on Cause)

Directions: Fill in the following chart, which is based on the preceding model paragraph.

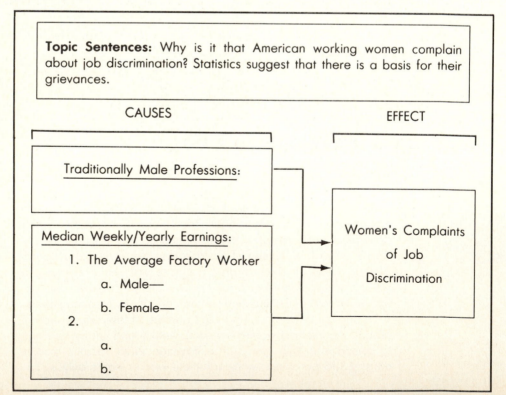

EXERCISE 5–6

Paragraph Writing:
Cause-Effect Information Transfer

Directions: Working alone, in pairs, or in small groups, study the cause-effect diagram. Then, on a separate sheet of paper, recopy the paragraph, filling in all the blanks. Some blanks will require only one word; others will require more than one. Before you begin, familiarize yourself with the meaning of the following terms:

a VCR
represents
factors
overwhelming popularity

(a) button
. . . , say, ...
a video club

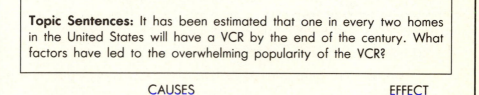

Topic Sentences: It has been estimated that one in every two homes in the United States will have a VCR by the end of the century. What factors have led to the overwhelming popularity of the VCR?

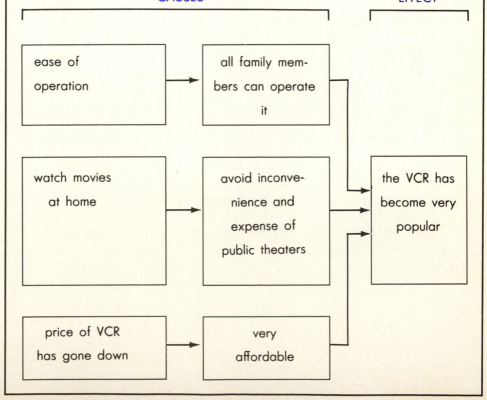

It has been estimated that one in every two homes in the United States will have a VCR by the end of the century. What factors have led to the overwhelming popularity of the VCR? Probably the major reason for its success is the fact that it is _____ to _____. This means that it (operate, can) _____ by every _____ of the _____; as a matter of fact, even young children (figure out, can) _____ which button (push) _____ to enable them (watch) _____ a movie. The second reason for the VCR's _____ is the fact that it saves time and _____. People _____ regularly watch movies in the comfort of _____ own homes have found that it is much more _____ and much less _____ than (have) _____ (go) _____ out to public theatres. As a matter of fact, (stay) _____ at home represents quite a savings for, say, a family of four: as little _____ $2.00 per movie at a video club, compared to the $25.00 it (require, usually) _____ (take) _____ the family to a theater. Finally, VCRs (be, not) _____ nearly as expensive _____ they used to be; and because they cost so much less _____ they used to, almost everyone (afford, now, can) _____ the pleasure and convenience of (watch) _____ movies at home.

EXERCISE 5–7

Paragraph Writing:
Cause-Effect (Focus on Cause)

Phase 1: Exploring Your Topic

Directions: Select one of the following topics and write down all the reasons you can think of. From this list, select the three reasons which you consider most significant. Then, write a topic sentence indicating that you will explain these reasons. If you are working with a partner or in groups, you may wish to show your topic sentence to your classmates to see if it is appropriate for the reasons you plan to write about.

General Topic

Explain why you decided to study at this school. (You may wish to reread the model paragraph in Unit 1 (page 10) before beginning this assignment.)

Essay Question

Discuss the reasons why the government of a developing country would want to send students abroad to study.

Phase 2: Writing the First Draft

Directions: Write the first draft of a paragraph in which you focus on causes. When you have finished, you may wish to show your paragraph to a classmate to see if you have developed the cause-effect relationship clearly.

Phase 3: Making Your Language Accurate

Directions: After you have revised your paragraph based on your classmate's suggestions, you will want to check it for correct usage. Proofread the paragraph to make sure that the **subjects** and **verbs** and **singular-plural** forms agree and that you have used appropriate **tenses** and **pronouns.** After you have corrected any errors, recopy this draft of your paragraph and submit it to your teacher.

Cause-Effect Development:
Chain Reaction

In developing a causal relationship, you will frequently find that the effect of one situation becomes the cause of the next. You have already seen a very good example of this—the paragraph dealing with the results of the Greenhouse Effect (page 96). When this relationship exists, we have what is called a *chain reaction.* In other words, the first event leads to or influences the second, the second leads to or influences the third, and so on.

Model Paragraph

For some time now, medical scientists have noted an alarming increase in diseases of the heart and circulation among people who smoke cigarettes. It has been found that the presence of nicotine in the bloodstream causes blood vessels to contract, thus slowing circulation, a condition which eventually leads to hardening of the arteries. As the arteries stiffen, less blood reaches the brain, and the end result of this slowdown is a cerebral hemorrhage, commonly referred to as a stroke. In addition, nicotine in the bloodstream reduces the ability of the hemoglobin to release oxygen, resulting in shortness of breath, thus causing the person to breathe more rapidly. This forces the heart to beat faster—that is, the pulse rate increases— and in turn accelerates the risk of a heart attack.

Now Ask Yourself ❧

1. What is the first cause in the chain?_____

2. What are the *two* final effects? (Notice that there are two chain reactions, both caused by nicotine in the bloodstream.)

_____

3. What time words, sentence connectors, or listing signals are used?

_____

_____

_____

EXERCISE 5–8

Analyzing a Chain-Reaction Paragraph

Topic Sentence: For some time now, medical scientists have noted an alarming increase in diseases of the heart and circulation among people who smoke cigarettes.

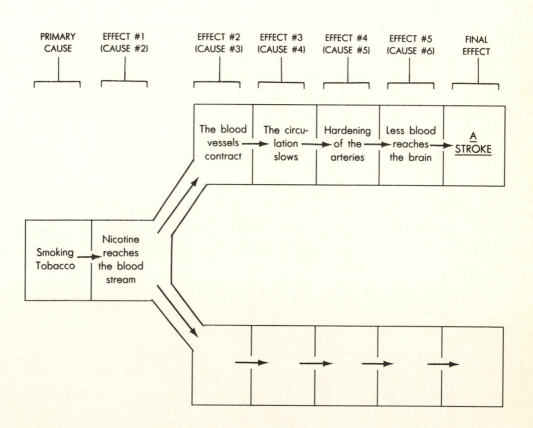

EXERCISE 5–9

Unscrambling a Chain-Reaction Paragraph

Directions: The following is a random list of causes and effects. Arrange them in the correct order, writing out the paragraph on a separate sheet of paper. Start your paragraph with the following topic sentence: *For some time now, medical scientists have noted an alarming increase in diseases of the lungs and respiratory tract among people who smoke cigarettes.* When you are satisfied with you paragraph, fill in the following chain reaction diagram.

1. Impurities can now collect in the windpipe, larynx, and lungs.

2. In addition to cancer, the lungs may lose their elasticity and cease to function efficiently.

3. The smoke slows the action of the tiny hairlike projections *(cilia)* which cleanse the air in the windpipe.

4. Precancerous and cancerous cells form in the various parts of the respiratory tract.

5. Smoke is inhaled.

6. With this loss of elasticity, emphysema may develop.

7. Moreover, since gas, tar, and smoke are no longer removed, they are now allowed to pass through the respiratory tract.

Topic Sentence: For some time now, medical scientists have noted an alarming increase in diseases of the lungs and respiratory tract among people who smoke cigarettes.

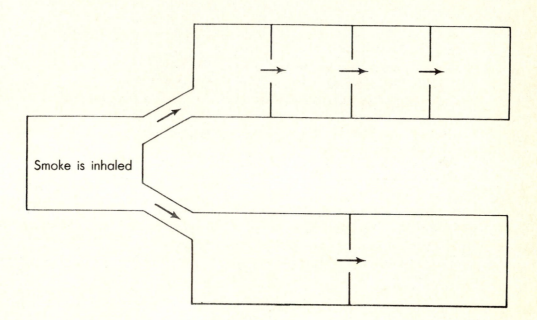

Smoke is inhaled

6

COMPARISON AND CONTRAST

You may also support your topic sentences by arranging the supporting sentences according to either the *similarities* or the *differences* between two things, or between two aspects of one thing.

COMPARISON: pointing out *likenesses*
CONTRAST: pointing out *differences*

In this unit, we will examine several of the ways in which comparative and contrastive paragraphs can be organized. We will first take a look at comparison.

Comparison

In the model paragraph which follows, notice that only similarities, or parallels, between the life and death of Kennedy and Lincoln are mentioned. There are obviously many differences between these two men, but the purpose of the paragraph, as it is stated in the topic sentence, is to show the likenesses or similarities between them. In a paragraph of comparison, the differences are often mentioned *only briefly* or are even *omitted entirely.*

Model Paragraph

[1]Are you aware of the striking similarities between two of the most popular U.S. presidents, Abraham Lincoln and John F. Kennedy? [2]A minor point is that the names Lincoln and Kennedy both have seven letters. [3]Both men had their elections legally challenged. [4]Lincoln and Kennedy are both remembered for their sense of humor, as well as for their interest in civil rights. [5]Lincoln became president in 1860; Kennedy, in 1960. [6]Lincoln's secretary was Mrs. Kennedy; Kennedy's secretary was Mrs. Lincoln. [7]Neither man took the advice of his secretary not to make a public appearance on the day on which he was assassinated. [8]Lincoln and Kennedy were both killed on a Friday in the presence of their wives. [9]Both assassins, John Wilkes Booth and Lee Harvey Oswald, have fifteen letters in their names, and both were murdered before they could be brought to trial. [10]Just as Lincoln was succeeded by a Southern Democrat named Johnson, so was Kennedy. [11]Andrew Johnson (Lincoln's successor) was born in 1808; Lyndon Johnson (Kennedy's successor) was born in 1908. [12]And finally, the same caisson carried the bodies of both men in their funeral processions.

Now Ask Yourself

1. Why are no differences mentioned in the paragraph?_____
   _____

2. What is the one key word in the topic sentence which controls the development of the paragraph?_____

3. What two words are repeated continually?_____

4. Do you find any examples of pronoun reference? Underline all pronouns and draw arrows to the words they represent.

5. What enumerators and listing signals have been used?
   _____

EXERCISE 6–1

Analyzing a Comparative Paragraph

Directions: Reread the model paragraph carefully. Then, in the following chart, indicate the *basis of comparison* in each sentence (that is, tell which similarity is being discussed) as well as the *comparative words* which have been used.

SENTENCE	BASIS OF COMPARISON	COMPARATIVE STRUCTURES
2	Number of letters in their names	The names Kennedy and Lincoln both have
3	Elections challenged	Both men
4		
5		
6		
7		
8		
9		
10		
11		
12		

STRUCTURES OF COMPARISON

In addition to *listing signals* and the enumerator *similarities*, certain other basic structures are used commonly in writing paragraphs of comparison. There are six basic types.

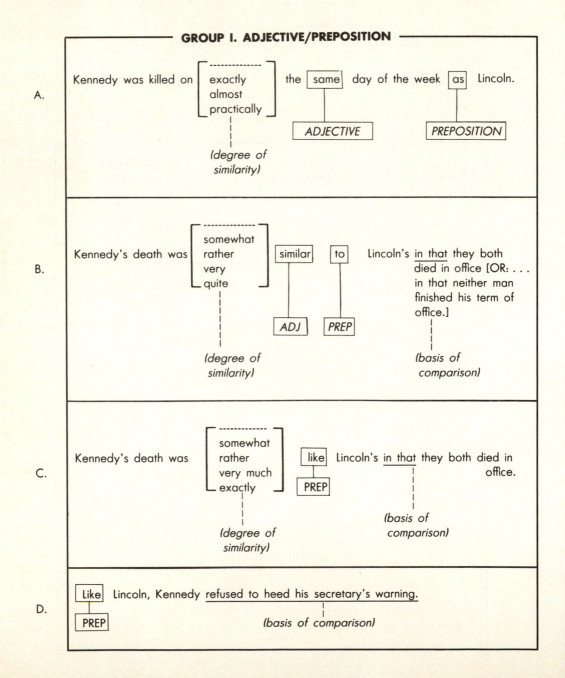

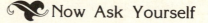

Now Ask Yourself

1. Which of the preceding structures do *not* contain adjectives?_____

2. What is the difference between *same* and *similar?*_____
_____

3. Which structure allows for the possibility of an *introductory* prepositional
phrase?_____

━ GROUP II. ATTACHED STATEMENTS ━

A.

Kennedy was succeeded by a Southern Democrat,	[and] Lincoln was [too.] / [and so] was Lincoln.
Kennedy could arouse the sympathy of the public,	[and] Lincoln could [too.] / [and so] could Lincoln.
Mrs. Kennedy witnessed her husband's assassination,	[and] Mrs. Lincoln did [too.] / [and so] did Mrs. Lincoln.

B.

Kennedy's assassin was not brought to trial,	[and] Lincoln's wasn't [either.] / [and neither] was Lincoln's.
Kennedy's secretary couldn't prevent the president's assassination,	[and] Lincoln's couldn't [either.] / [and neither] could Lincoln's.
Kennedy didn't finish his term of office,	[and] Lincoln didn't [either.] / [and neither] did Lincoln.

Now Ask Yourself

1. What kinds of statements are joined by *and . . . too* and *and so?*_____
What happens to the second subject and verb when *and so* is used?
_____

2. What kinds of statements are joined by *and . . . either* and *and neither?*
_____

What happens to the second subject and verb when *and neither* is used?
_____

3. What part of the verb is repeated in the second part of the statement

   if there is an auxiliary *was?*_____

   if the auxiliary is *could?*_____

   if there is no auxiliary?_____

4. Rewrite one of the sentences in both A and B (page 121), using Group I signals.

   a. _____ was similar to _____ in that ____

   _____

   b. _____ was similar to _____ in that ____

   _____

GROUP III. CORRELATIVE CONJUNCTIONS

A.

| Both | Kennedy | and | Lincoln |
| Kennedy | and | Lincoln | both |

had their elections legally challenged.

B.

| Neither | Kennedy's wife | nor | his children were expecting anything unusual to happen that day.

| Neither | Kennedy's children | nor | his wife was expecting anything unusual to happen that day.

C.

| Just as | Lincoln died in office, | so | Kennedy was still president when he was assassinated.

Note: In the **just as ··· so** *structures, the wording in the sentence following* **so** *should be slightly different to avoid repetition.*

Now Ask Yourself

1. In the example sentences for *neither . . . nor,* why are the verbs different *(was, were)?*_____

2. Rewrite the sentences from A, B, and C (above) using Group II signals. Be sure to punctuate correctly.

   A. Kennedy had his_____

   and so_____.

B. Kennedy's wife_____

and his children_____.

C. Lincoln_____

and Kennedy_____.

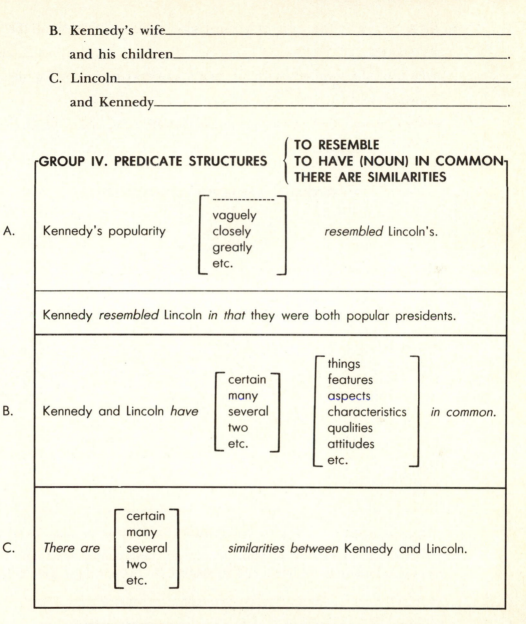

GROUP IV. PREDICATE STRUCTURES { TO RESEMBLE / TO HAVE (NOUN) IN COMMON / THERE ARE SIMILARITIES

A. Kennedy's popularity [vaguely / closely / greatly / etc.] *resembled* Lincoln's.

Kennedy *resembled* Lincoln *in that* they were both popular presidents.

B. Kennedy and Lincoln *have* [certain / many / several / two / etc.] [things / features / aspects / characteristics / qualities / attitudes / etc.] *in common.*

C. *There are* [certain / many / several / two / etc.] *similarities between* Kennedy and Lincoln.

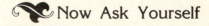 Now Ask Yourself

1. Which of the preceding structures seems most appropriate for showing a *single* similarity?_____

2. Which might make a better topic sentence for a paragraph which includes *many* areas of comparison?_____ _____

3. In A, where is the *basis* of comparison indicated in each of the two

sentences?_____

Which of the two seems to be more appropriate for giving detailed

information?_____

Why? (Can you think of a *grammatical* reason?)_____

_____

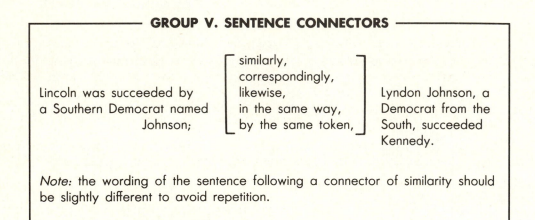

GROUP V. SENTENCE CONNECTORS

Lincoln was succeeded by a Southern Democrat named Johnson;

[similarly, correspondingly, likewise, in the same way, by the same token,]

Lyndon Johnson, a Democrat from the South, succeeded Kennedy.

Note: the wording of the sentence following a connector of similarity should be slightly different to avoid repetition.

Now Ask Yourself

1. Rewrite this sentence, using one of the suggested connectors, as two separate sentences.

_____

_____

2. From the point of view of punctuation, do these connectors remind you of any others that we have studied so far? Be precise: Give examples.

_____

_____

GROUP VI. PUNCTUATION ONLY

A.   Andrew Johnson was born in 1808; Lyndon Johnson was born in 1908.

B.   Andrew Johnson was born in 1808; Lyndon Johnson, in 1908.

Now Ask Yourself

What missing element does the comma replace in sentence B?

_____

_____

EXERCISE 6–2

Paraphrasing Sentences of Comparison

Directions: The following sentences are based on the model paragraph (the similarities between Lincoln and Kennedy). Rewrite each of the sentences in two different ways, using the words or phrases which have been indicated. Pay attention to *punctuation*.

1. A minor point is that the names Kennedy and Lincoln both have seven letters.

   (and so/and . . . too)_____

   _____

   (both . . . and)_____

   _____

2. John Wilkes Booth and Lee Harvey Oswald were murdered before they could be brought to trial.

   (Neither . . . nor)_____

   _____

   (like . . . in that)_____

   _____

3. Neither man took the advice of his secretary on the day when he was killed.

   (and neither/and . . . either)_____

   _____

   (similarly)_____

   _____

4. The same caisson carried the bodies of both men in their funeral processions.

   (similar to . . . in that)_____

   _____

(Hint: make *funeral* procession the subject.)

(resembled . . . in that)_____

_____

5. Lincoln became president in 1860; Kennedy, in 1960.

(similar to . . . in that)_____

_____

(similarly)_____

_____

6. Lincoln's secretary was Mrs. Kennedy, and Kennedy's secretary was Mrs. Lincoln.

(just as . . . so)_____

_____

(;)_____

_____

EXERCISE 6–3

Guided Paragraph Writing: Comparative Information Transfer

Directions: Working alone, in pairs, or in small groups, study the following notes, which are given in list form. Then, on a separate sheet of paper, recopy the paragraph, filling in all the blanks. Some blanks will require only one word; others will require more than one. Before you begin, familiarize yourself with the meanings of the words in the list.

Humans and Chimpanzees (Bases of Comparison)

1. Biological Classification
   both are classified as primates

2. Skeleton
   skeletal structure generally similar
   five fingers on each hand
   a movable thumb that allows the hand to grasp objects

3. Locomotion
   chimpanzees most often travel using all four limbs, but can walk upright
   humans walk upright (on two legs)

4. Offspring (Young)
   number: not as many as other mammals
   gestation: about nine months
   care: several years (necessary for learning essential survival skills)

5. Intelligence
   curiosity: both like to discover new things
   language ability: use of abstract symbols to communicate; humans use words, can invent new combinations; chimpanzees can learn to use body signs and can invent new combinations

Although humans and chimpanzees do not seem very much alike at first glance, they are both classified as primates and thus share a number of remarkably similar characteristics. First of all, the skeletons of humans and chimpanzees are quite _____; _____ species possess five fingers on each hand, (include) _____ a movable thumb which makes the hand capable of (grasp) _____ objects. Although chimpanzees (prefer, travel) _____ on all fours, they (be able, walk) _____ upright _____ humans. Female chimpanzees have fewer young _____ other mammals, and humans do, _____. The young of the _____ species are born after a gestation period of about _____ months and then stay with their mothers for several years, a period which (permit, them, learn) _____ what they need to know in order (survive) _____. But of all the _____ between the two species, perhaps the most notable is their intelligence. Just as humans enjoy (discover) _____ new things, _____ chimpanzees are quite curious about what they (know, not) _____. Even more important here is the question of language ability. Although the sounds which (make) _____ by chimpanzees (resemble, not, really) _____ those made by humans, many experts believe that there is a real _____ in the way both species can use abstract symbols to communicate meanings. Humans communicate with each other through words; _____ , it (believe) _____ that chimpanzees (can, teach) _____ to communicate by means of *signs,* another variety of abstract symbols. Moreover, chimps (seem, possess) _____ the _____ to learn a rather large vocabulary of signs and then to put these signs together in entirely new combinations—an ability which closely (resemble) _____ what humans do with words. In other words, humans can be creative in the way they communicate, and so _____ chimpanzees.

EXERCISE 6–4

Paragraph Writing: Comparison

Phase 1: Exploring Your Topic

Directions: Select one of the following topics and write down all the points of similarity you can think of. From this list, select the three points which you consider most significant. Then write a topic sentence indicating that you will describe these similarities. If you are working with a partner or in groups, you may wish to show your topic sentence to your classmates to see if it is appropriate for the similarities which you plan to write about.

General Topic

Compare two people you know who are very similar in appearance and/or personality.

Essay Question

Compare two products (automobiles, soft drinks, stereo systems, and so forth) which are similar.

Phase 2: Writing the First Draft

Directions: Write the first draft of a paragraph in which you focus on similarities. When you have finished, you may wish to show your paragraph to a classmate to see if you have developed the points of similarity clearly.

Phase 3: Making Your Language Accurate

Directions: After you have revised your paragraph based on your classmate's suggestions, you will want to check it for correct usage. Proofread the paragraph to make sure that the **subjects** and **verbs** and **singular-plural** forms agree and that you have used appropriate **tenses** and **pronouns.**

Another common usage error is writing **run-on sentences.** This involves writing two sentences as one and frequently occurs when the ideas in both sentences are closely related. Notice the examples of this type of error in the following sentences.

Abraham Lincoln is remembered for his sense of humor **and** John Kennedy is, too.

There are two complete sentences written as one in the preceding example. It can be corrected either by putting a **period** after *humor* or by combining the two sentences by putting a **comma** after *humor* and adding the **conjunction** *and*.

Lincoln was assassinated on a Friday in the presence of his wife. Mrs. Kennedy was with her husband on the Friday when he was killed.

There are two complete sentences written as one in this example. It can be corrected by using a **period** or a **semicolon** instead of a comma after *wife*.

Proofread your paragraph again to make sure that you have not written any **run-on sentences.** After you have corrected any errors, recopy this draft of your paragraph and submit it to your teacher.

Contrast

Notice that in the following model paragraph, the author concentrates on the *differences* between extreme extroversion and extreme introversion. He has not denied, however, that most people are a combination of both of these; on the contrary, the expression *a scale* suggests precisely such a combination.

Model Paragraph

[1]According to the Swiss psychiatrist Carl Gustav Jung, every person's personality can be placed somewhere on a scale running from extreme *extroversion* (an outgoing personality) to extreme *introversion* (a withdrawn personality). [2]The typical extrovert is particularly fond of people and people-oriented activities: he or she is sociable, likes parties, has many friends, needs to have people to talk to, and does not like reading or studying alone. [3]The typical introvert, on the other hand, is a quiet, retiring sort of person, introspective, fond of books rather

than people. ⁴Unlike the extrovert, who craves excitement, takes chances, and is generally impulsive, the introvert shuns excitement, takes matters of everyday life with proper seriousness, and likes a well-ordered mode of life. ⁵Whereas the extrovert tends to be aggressive and loses his or her temper easily, the introvert tends to keep his or her feelings under close control, seldom behaves in an aggressive manner, and does not lose his or her temper easily. ⁶The introvert is more reliable and less optimistic than the extrovert. ⁷The extrovert may often be subject to criminal or psychopathic behavior, in contrast to the introvert, who may exhibit neurotic tendencies. ⁸A further difference between the two involves the ability to remember: Studies have tended to show that the extrovert learns faster than the introvert but, in the end, remembers less.[1]

Now Ask Yourself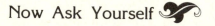

1. Why are no similarities mentioned in the model paragraph?_____

   _____

2. What part of the topic sentence prepares the reader to expect a paragraph

   of contrast development?_____

3. What two words are repeated continually?_____ _____

4. Do you find any examples of pronoun reference? Underline all pronouns and draw arrows to the words they represent.

5. Are any *listing signals* and *enumerators* used?_____

EXERCISE 6–5

Analyzing a Paragraph of Contrast

Directions: Reread the sample paragraph carefully. Then, in the following chart, indicate which contrast words have been used for each area of contrast. Also note briefly the differences themselves.

---

[1] Nicholas Wright, ed., *Understanding Human Behaviour* (London: Phoebus Publishing Company/BPC Publishing, Limited, 1974), pp. 54–56.

SENTENCE	BASES OF CONTRAST		CONTRASTIVE STRUCTURES
	Extrovert	*Introvert*	
2,3	(Sociability)		On the other hand
	Fond of people: sociable, likes parties, etc.	Prefers books to people, is shy and retiring	
4	(Risk-taking)		
5	(Expression of feelings, aggression)		
6	(Reliability, optimism)		
7	( )		
8	( )		

Structures of Contrast

┌─GROUP I. -ER . . . THAN; MORE . . . THAN; LESS . . . THAN; AS . . . AS─┐

A.
1.
The introvert

⎡ is quieter than
is *more* reliable *than*
is *less* optimistic *than*
learns *more* slowly *than* ⎤

2.
the extrovert.

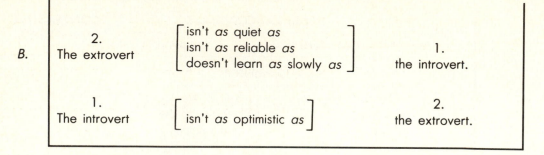

B. The extrovert
[
isn't *as* quiet *as*
isn't *as* reliable *as*
doesn't learn *as* slowly *as*
]
the introvert.

The introvert
[
isn't *as* optimistic *as*
]
the extrovert.

Now Ask Yourself

1. What kinds of words are used with *-er . . . than?*_____

   With *more . . . than* and *less . . . than?*_____

2. When can *as . . . as* be used to indicate contrast? (Remember that it can
   also indicate similarity.) _____

3. On a separate sheet of paper, rewrite all the sentences in A and B, keeping
   the meaning the same but changing the order of *extrovert* and *introvert*.
   (For example, "The extrovert is . . .")

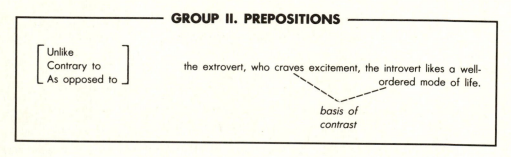

GROUP II. PREPOSITIONS

[
Unlike
Contrary to
As opposed to
]
the extrovert, who craves excitement, the introvert likes a well-
ordered mode of life.

*basis of
contrast*

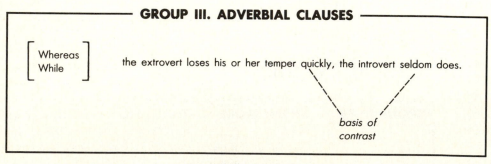

GROUP III. ADVERBIAL CLAUSES

[
Whereas
While
]
the extrovert loses his or her temper quickly, the introvert seldom does.

*basis of
contrast*

Now Ask Yourself

Rewrite the sentence in the following ways:

1. The introvert_____ ,

whereas the extrovert_____ .

2. Unlike the_____, who _____

_____, the _____ .

— GROUP IV. VERBAL STRUCTURES —

The introvert ⌈ contrasts *with* ⌉ the extrovert { in regard to } his or her temper.
⎜ differs *from* ⎜ { in respect to }
⌊ is different *from* ⌋

basis of contrast

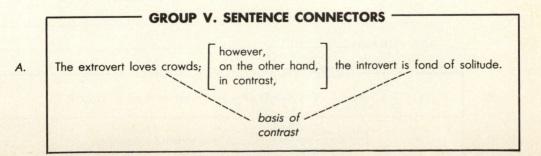 Now Ask Yourself

1. Can the basis of contrast be explained more fully by using a structure from this group or by using an adverbial clause, as was done in Group III?

_____

2. Can the basis of contrast be explained more fully by using *in that* instead of *in regard to?*_____

_____

3. Rewrite the sentence from the preceding box, combining Group III and Group IV signals with *in that.*

"The introvert _____ from the extrovert in that the extrovert

_____, whereas

the introvert _____."

Note: A comma is used before the contrast signals *whereas* and *while.*

— GROUP V. SENTENCE CONNECTORS —

A.   The extrovert loves crowds; ⌈ however, ⌉ the introvert is fond of solitude.
⎜ on the other hand, ⎜
⌊ in contrast, ⌋

basis of contrast

B.   The extrovert loves crowds; the introvert, [however, on the other hand, in contrast,] is fond of solitude.

Now Ask Yourself

1. How does the punctuation of the preceding two sentences differ?_____

_____

2. Rewrite *each* of them as two separate sentences.

a. _____

_____

b. _____

_____

GROUP VI. CONJUNCTIONS

The extrovert loves crowds, [but] the introvert is fond of solitude.

(basis of contrast)

Now Ask Yourself

1. Can the order extrovert/introvert be reversed without a change in meaning?
2. Rewrite the sentence in the following three ways:

a. The introvert _____ the extrovert, however_____.

b. The extrovert contrasts _____ the introvert in regard to _____.

c. _____ the introvert, who _____, the extrovert_____.

GROUP VII. PUNCTUATION ONLY

A.   The introvert likes books; the extrovert is fond of people.

B.   The introvert likes books; the extrovert, people.

EXERCISE 6–6

Paraphrasing Sentences of Contrast

Directions: The following sentences are based on the model paragraph (the differences between the typical extrovert and the typical introvert). Rewrite each of the sentences in two different ways, using words or phrases from the sentence, as well as the structure of contrast which has been indicated. Refer back to the boxes on the preceding pages as often as necessary. Pay attention to *punctuation.*

1. Studies have tended to show that the extrovert learns faster than the introvert but, in the end, remembers less.

    (however,—form B) Studies have tended to show that the extrovert learns faster than the introvert; in the end, however, he or she remembers less.

    (while) _____

    _____

    _____

2. Unlike the extrovert, who takes chances and is generally impulsive, the introvert shuns excitement.

    (differs from . . . in that . . . whereas) _____

    _____

    _____

    (more/-er . . . than) _____

    _____

3. The typical extrovert is particularly fond of parties and people-oriented activities; in contrast, the typical introvert is a quiet, introspective sort of person.

    (unlike . . . who)_____

    _____

    _____

    (while)_____

    _____

    _____

4. The extrovert may be subject to criminal or psychopathic behavior, in contrast to the introvert, who may exhibit neurotic tendencies.

(differ from . . . in that . . . whereas) _____

_____

(on the other hand—form B) _____

_____

5. Whereas the extrovert tends to be aggressive and loses his or her temper quickly, the introvert seldom behaves in an aggressive manner and keeps his or her feelings under close control.

(unlike . . . who)_____

_____

_____

(contrast with . . . in regard to)_____

_____

_____

Methods of Contrast

There are two main ways in which to organize your material when you wish to develop a contrast paragraph. The first method has been used in the preceding model paragraph (the typical extrovert versus the typical introvert). In this method, the contrasts are made one at a time, or *point-by-point*. Thus, the two personality types are first contrasted for sociability, then for risk taking, and so on. Note, in the preceding model paragraph, that the words *extrovert* and *introvert* are repeated each time a new area of contrast is mentioned.

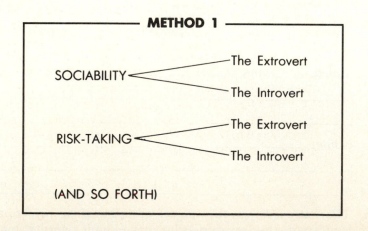

The writer could, of course, have *completely described* the extrovert, then, in the second part of the paragraph, gone on to *completely describe* the introvert. This would have given a very different-looking, but equally acceptable, paragraph:

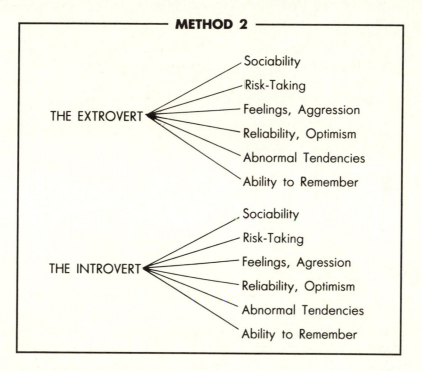

METHOD 2

THE EXTROVERT
- Sociability
- Risk-Taking
- Feelings, Aggression
- Reliability, Optimism
- Abnormal Tendencies
- Ability to Remember

THE INTROVERT
- Sociability
- Risk-Taking
- Feelings, Agression
- Reliability, Optimism
- Abnormal Tendencies
- Ability to Remember

The following is an example of Method 2 (completely describing one thing, then completely describing the other):

In studying the phenomenon usually referred to as sleep, we are actually dealing with more than one phenomenon. In fact, we spend the night alternating between two different types of sleep, each with different brain mechanisms and different purposes. As people fall asleep, their brain waves develop a slower and less regular pattern than in a waking state. This is called *orthodox* sleep. In this state, the brain is apparently resting. Its blood supply is reduced, and its temperature falls slightly. Breathing and heart rate are regular. The muscles remain slightly tensed. After about an hour in this state, however, the brain waves begin to show a more active pattern again, even though people are apparently asleep very deeply. This is called *paradoxical* sleep, because it has much in common with being awake. Paradoxical (active) sleep is marked by irregular breathing and heart rate, increased blood supply to the brain, and increased brain temperature. Most of the muscles are relaxed.

There are various jerky movements of the body and face, including short bursts of rapid eye movement (REMs), which indicate that we are dreaming. Thus, we spend the night alternating between these two vital restoration jobs: working on the brain (paradoxical sleep) and working on the body (orthodox sleep.)[2]

Now Ask Yourself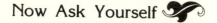

1. Is the *first* or the *second* sentence the topic sentence? Or is it *both* of them? (Explain your answer.)_____

   _____

   _____

2. What *contrast structures* do you find in the paragraph?_____

   _____

   Which type of contrast—Method 1 or Method 2—seems to require more

   structures of contrast? _____ Why? _____

   _____

3. Are all of the following bases of contrast referred to in both orthodox and paradoxical sleep? Check each box as you find the information. Two boxes should be empty.

	ORTHODOX	PARADOXICAL
Brain waves (speed and regularity)		
Amount of blood (blood supply)		
Temperature		
Breathing, heart rate		
Muscle tension		
Body and face movements		
Rapid eye movements		

   If you were writing a contrastive paragraph but did not have complete information on one of the things you were contrasting, which method would you choose? Why?_____

   _____

[2] Ibid., pp. 23–24.

ADDITIONAL COMMENTS ON THE TOPIC SENTENCE

You were told in Unit 1 that most paragraphs begin with a topic sentence (see page 3). However, since then you have seen two examples of something you will encounter in English—*two* beginning sentences which carry the main idea of the paragraph. The first paragraph was on page 107.

> Why is it that American working women complain about job discrimination? Statistics suggest that there is a basis for their grievances.

_____

_____

_____

_____

_____

_____

You will notice that the first sentence introduces the idea in a general way, wondering why women complain. The second sentence goes further and notes that there *are* reasons, and that these reasons are verifiable through statistics. The paragraph then goes on to present these statistics to the reader.

At this point, there is no reason why you should try to write paragraphs which begin with these double topic sentences. Nevertheless, you must learn to be aware of them while you are reading; otherwise, you may miss the point which the author is trying to make.

EXERCISE 6–7

Analyzing Paragraphs of Contrast

Directions: Read the paragraph on the two types of sleep again carefully, and then fill in the following chart in a fairly detailed fashion.

TOPIC SENTENCES	
ORTHODOX SLEEP	Brain waves—slower, less regular
	Blood supply
	Temperature
	Breathing, heart rate
	Muscle tension
	Body and face movements
	Rapid eye movements
PARADOXICAL SLEEP	Brain waves
	Blood supply
	Temperature
	Breathing, heart rate
	Muscle tension
	Body and face movements
	Rapid eye movements
CONCLUSION	

EXERCISE 6–8

Reordering Paragraphs of Contrast

Directions: Take the paragraph on sleep (Method 2) and rewrite it according to Method 1 (point-by-point). Use as many contrast expressions as necessary.

EXERCISE 6–9

Analyzing and Reordering Paragraphs of Contrast

Directions: Read the following paragraph, which is organized according to Method 1 (point-by-point). Fill in the chart that follows. Then rewrite the paragraph according to Method 2 (completely describe the first; then completely describe the second).

[1]Although the classless society is still a myth, the distinctions and barriers between classes are fewer in the United States than in many more traditional parts of the world. [2]Whereas in the old world, class is legal and hereditary, in the United States it is neither. [3]In the old world, too, it is quite impersonal: you are what you are, and that is the end of it. [4]On the contrary, in America it is wholly personal; each person carves out an economic position, just as he or she carves out a social position. [5]Nor is the job ever finished once and for all; as the individual can move upward on the social scale, so he or she can move downward. [6]In the United States neither wealth, family, nor formal position provides any guarantee, though collectively they do provide indications of social standing. [7]In parts of Europe and Asia, a government official has a kind of automatic right to deference and prestige and is deemed worthy of respect until proved otherwise. [8]The opposite is true in America. [9]One does not command respect or honor merely on the basis of title; it is well to remember that the title of the President of the United States is "Mr. President." [10]A judge may be "Your Honor" and a clergyman "Reverend," but the judge will not receive honor nor the clergyman reverence unless he or she merits it. [11]Money can, of course, buy special favors—the best seats in a restaurant, the best service in a hotel—but it cannot buy deference. [12]In other lands, too, class commonly has outward symbols: dress, manner, speech, accent, school, church affiliation, unlike the U.S., where these indices are of little or no importance, and anyone who tried to apply them would go badly astray.[3]

[3] Adapted from Henry Steel Commager, *Meet the U.S.A.* (New York: Institute of International Education, 1970), p. 87.

SENTENCE	BASES OF CONTRAST		GRAMMATICAL STRUCTURE(S)
	The old world	The United States	
2	(Nature of Class)		whereas
	Legal, hereditary	Neither legal nor hereditary	
3,4,5,6	(Personal versus Impersonal; Stability)		
7,8,9, 10,11	(Title versus Respect)		
12	(Visible Symbols of Class)		

EXERCISE 6–10

Paragraph Writing:
Contrastive Information Transfer

Directions: Working alone, in pairs, or in groups, study the graph. Then, copy the paragraph on a separate sheet of paper, filling in all the blanks. Some blanks will require only one word; others will require more than one.

Bar Graphs. The following graph is called a *bar graph*, since information is represented by bars which indicate a certain quantity of something or a certain number of things. This particular graph is a *double* bar graph, and this makes it a useful kind of visual aid to use when it is necessary to contrast two different things.

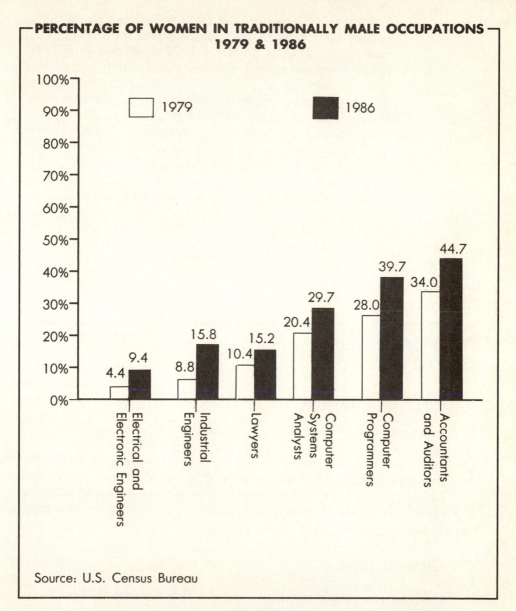

PERCENTAGE OF WOMEN IN TRADITIONALLY MALE OCCUPATIONS 1979 & 1986

☐ 1979   ■ 1986

Occupation	1979	1986
Electrical and Electronic Engineers	4.4	9.4
Industrial Engineers	8.8	15.8
Lawyers	10.4	15.2
Computer Systems Analysts	20.4	29.7
Computer Programmers	28.0	39.7
Accountants and Auditors	34.0	44.7

Source: U.S. Census Bureau

Although women can still rightfully complain about inequities in the hiring practices of many companies, they can find hope in at least one major change that has been occurring since 1979: many higher-paid occupations are now hiring more and more women for jobs that used to be reserved exclusively for men. For example, _____ only 34 percent of accountants and auditors were women in 1979, by 1986 that figure (increase)

_____ to 44.7 percent. This trend (seem, take place) _____ in many other fields as well. The proportion of female _____ (rise) _____ from 28 percent in 1979 to 40 percent in 1986, female computer systems analysts _____ 20.4 _____ 29.7 _____, and _____ from _____ to _____ percent. Even the field of engineering, once almost exclusively male-dominated, (show) _____ a _____ -er percentage of _____ in _____ than it _____. In 1979, women represented only 8.8 percent of all industrial engineers, _____ by 1986 that number (climb) _____ to 15.8 percent. An increase (notice, also, can) _____ with regard to _____ engineers: _____ percent of them were women in _____, as compared to only _____ in _____.

NOTE: Whereas and _while_ should each be used once in the paragraph.

EXERCISE 6–11

Paragraph Writing: Contrast

Phase 1: Exploring Your Topic

Directions: Select one of the following topics and write down all of the differences you can think of about it. From this list, select the three differences which you consider most significant. Then, write a topic sentence indicating that you will describe these points of contrast. If you are working with a partner or in groups, you may wish to show your topic sentence to your classmates to see if it is appropriate for the differences you plan to write about.

General Topic

Contrast two people you know who are very different in appearance and/or personality.

Essay Question

Contrast the two products you wrote about in Exercise 6–4.

Phase 2: Writing the First Draft

Directions: Write the first draft of a paragraph in which you focus on differences. When you have finished, you may wish to show your paragraph to a classmate to see if you have developed the points of contrast clearly.

Phase 3: Making Your Language Accurate

Directions: After you have revised your paragraph based on your classmate's suggestions, you will want to check it for correct usage. Proofread the paragraph to make sure that the **subjects** and **verbs** and **singular-plural** forms agree, that you have used appropriate **tenses** and **pronouns,** and that you have not written any **run-on sentences.** After you have corrected any errors, recopy this draft of your paragraph and submit it to your teacher.

Comparison *and* Contrast

You have no doubt realized that when you are showing similarities between two things, you will almost always find differences as well. The converse is equally true: most things being contrasted will also have similarities. This is the case with the following model paragraphs.

Model Paragraphs

[1]When listening to a conversation between an American and an Englishman, a person will become aware of the most significant differences between the two varieties of the English language. [2]While the Englishman does not pronounce *r* sounds before a consonant sound or at the end of a word, the American does. [3]This might lead to a rather humorous misunderstanding if, when asked by the American what his job was, the Englishman answered that he was a *clerk* (pronounced *clock* to the American ear). [4]Failure to use the *r* sound at the end of a word might also lead to confusion between words like *paw* and *pour*. [5]Moreover, a noticeable difference exists between the basic words used to express the same thing. [6]The American might want to know the price of gas in London, but the Englishman will answer him by using the word *petrol*. [7]Unlike the American, who wears an *undershirt* when the weather is cold, the Englishman wears a *vest*. [8]The American wants to know where the *elevator* is, while the Englishman asks the location of the *lift*.

[9]The similarities found in this hypothetical conversation, however, will far outweigh the differences. [10]The meanings of most words are, of course, exactly the same. [11]The pronunciation of the consonant sounds, the rhythm, stress, and intonation systems in both American and British English closely resemble each other.

[12]In grammar, the similarities are numerous. [13]British English makes a distinction between count and mass nouns, and so does American English. [14]They both have the same verb and tense systems. [15]The grammar of both languages is similar in that they both form and compare adjectives and adverbs in the same way. [16]In fact, the similarities between the two languages—or, more precisely, between these two forms of the same language—are such that there is rarely any serious breakdown in communication between an American speaker and a British speaker.

EXERCISE 6–12

Analyzing Paragraphs of Comparison and Contrast

Directions: After carefully rereading the model paragraphs on the differences and similarities between American and British English, fill in the two charts which follow.

PARAGRAPH 1 (differences)

Topic Sentence: _____

_____

_____

SENTENCE	BASES OF CONTRAST		CONTRASTIVE STRUCTURES
	American	*British*	
2	*Pronunciation*		while
	r pronounced before consonants and at end of words	not pronounced	
3	(Example)		

4	(Example)	
5	*Certain Vocabulary Items*	
6	(Example)	
7	(Example)	
8	(Example)	

PARAGRAPH 2 (similarities)

Topic Sentence: _____

_____

_____

SENTENCE	BASIS OF COMPARISON	COMPARATIVE STRUCTURES
10		
11		

12		
13		
14		
15		

TOPIC SENTENCES OF COMPARISON *AND* CONTRAST

In the preceding exercise, you were asked to find a topic sentence for each of the two paragraphs. However, these two paragraphs *go* together, since their combined purpose is to show similarities *and* differences. Therefore, the meanings of their two topic sentences go together, even though they are separated physically from each other.

Remember This:

1. The main idea may be carried by *one* or *more* sentences.
2. They may be *together* (in the case of a single paragraph) or *split* (in the case of more than one paragraph).

Thus, the complete main idea for the preceding model paragraphs is as follows:

When listening to a conversation between an American and an Englishman, a person will become aware of the most significant differences between the two varieties of the English language..

_____

_____

_____

_____

The similarities found in this hypothetical conversation, however, will far outweigh the differences._____

_____

_____

_____

This is important for you to know, particularly when you are reading.
Otherwise, you might miss the fact that there are both similarities *and*
differences, and that the similarities are *far more numerous and important.*

EXERCISE 6–13

**Paragraph Writing:
Comparison *and* Contrast**

Phase 1: Exploring Your Topic

Directions: Select one of the following topics and write two lists—one of
similarities and the other of differences. From these lists, select the three
similarities and three differences which you consider most significant. Then,
formulate your two topic sentences. Decide whether the similarities or the
differences are more important; put the most important last (ascending order).
If you are working with a partner or in groups, you may wish to show your
split topic sentence to your classmates to see if it is appropriate for the
comparisons and contrasts you plan to write about.

General Topic

The similarities and differences between you and another member of your
family

Essay Question

Discuss the similarities and differences between (your native language) as it
is spoken in (your country) and as it is spoken in another country or in
another part of (your country). (You may wish to reread the model paragraph
on American and British forms of English, page 145, before you begin.)

Phase 2: Writing the First Draft

Directions: Write the first draft of two paragraphs in which you focus on comparisons and contrasts. Make sure that you give specific examples of each point that you make. When you have finished, you may wish to show your work to a classmate to see if you have developed the points of comparison and contrast clearly.

Phase 3: Making Your Language Accurate

Directions: After you have revised your work based on your classmate's suggestions, you will want to check it for correct usage. Proofread your work to make sure that the **subjects** and **verbs** and **singular-plural** forms agree, that you have used appropriate **tenses** and **pronouns,** and that you have not written any **run-on sentences.** After you have corrected any errors, recopy this draft of your work and submit it to your teacher.

7

DEFINITION

In formal writing, it is sometimes necessary to write a paragraph to explain what a term means or how you are using it in a particular situation. This is called a *paragraph of definition*. A paragraph of definition may be either a *formal* definition, which explains the meaning as you might find it in the dictionary, or a *stipulated* definition, which explains how you are using a particular term within a specific context. In both cases, you will notice that definition often involves a combination of the kinds of development we have been studying in the previous four units.

The Formal Definition

Model Definition

> A wristwatch is a mechanical time-telling device which is worn on a band about the wrist.

As you can see, a formal definition includes three kinds of things: the term to be defined, the class to which a thing belongs, and the features which distinguish it from other things in that class. In the case of a wristwatch:

Term = wristwatch

Class = device

Distinguishing features = (1) mechanical
(2) for telling time
(3) worn on a band about the wrist

Thus, it is distingished from nonmechanical time-telling devices (for example, sundials) and other kinds of mechanical ones (for example, alarm clocks).

A diagram of the information might look like this:

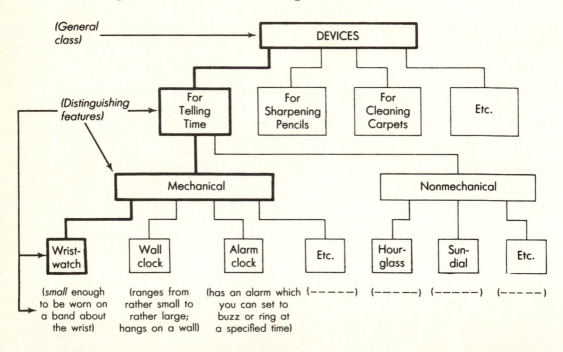

STRUCTURES OF DEFINITION

There are certain basic structures commonly used in writing definitions. They can be divided into two basic groups: those associated with distinguishing features and those associated with the choice of verb.

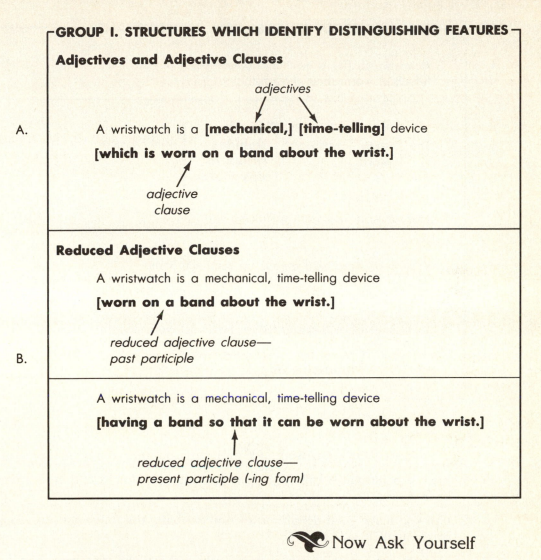

┌─ **GROUP I. STRUCTURES WHICH IDENTIFY DISTINGUISHING FEATURES** ─┐

Adjectives and Adjective Clauses

adjectives

A.   A wristwatch is a **[mechanical,] [time-telling]** device

[which is worn on a band about the wrist.]

*adjective
clause*

Reduced Adjective Clauses

A wristwatch is a mechanical, time-telling device

[worn on a band about the wrist.]

*reduced adjective clause—
past participle*

B.

A wristwatch is a mechanical, time-telling device

[having a band so that it can be worn about the wrist.]

*reduced adjective clause—
present participle (-ing form)*

🎐 Now Ask Yourself

1. How would you order the following elements? (Which comes first, which comes second, and so forth?)

____ adjective   ____ adjective clause   ____ noun (term)

2. How does a reduced adjective clause differ from a regular adjective clause?

_____

3. Can you make a good definition by unscrambling the following?
is / mechanical / which / an alarm clock / can be set to ring at a certain time / time-telling / a device

An alarm clock _____

_____

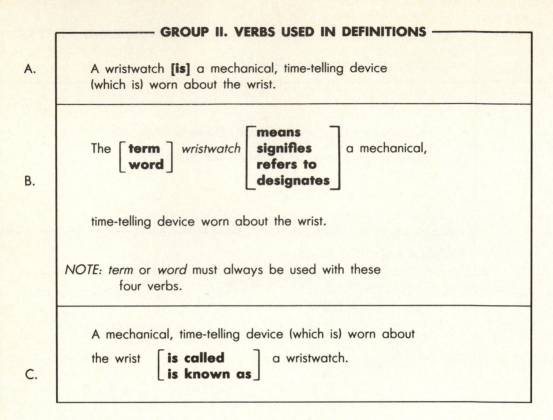

GROUP II. VERBS USED IN DEFINITIONS

A. A wristwatch **[is]** a mechanical, time-telling device (which is) worn about the wrist.

B. The [**term** / **word**] *wristwatch* [**means** / **signifies** / **refers to** / **designates**] a mechanical, time-telling device worn about the wrist.

NOTE: term or word must always be used with these four verbs.

C. A mechanical, time-telling device (which is) worn about the wrist [**is called** / **is known as**] a wristwatch.

Now Ask Yourself

1. How is definition A different from definition B? How is C different from both A and B?

2. Can you make good definitions by unscrambling the following two groups of elements?

   a device / a sundial / is known as / which shows the time by a shadow / time-telling / on a marked surface

   _____

   _____

   _____

   enclosed in a large wooden case / mechanical / *grandfather clock* / time-telling / worked by weights / refers to / the term / a device / and

   _____

   _____

   _____

EXERCISE 7–1

Combining Elements of Formal Definition

Directions: Working alone, in pairs, or in small groups, use the elements in the following chart to construct definitions, as has been done in the example. Try to use a variety of structures of definition.

Example

A mechanical time-telling device which is worn on a band about the wrist is known as a wristwatch.

TERM	GENERAL CLASS	DISTINGUISHING FEATURES
✓wristwatch	liquid	He has never been married.
orphan	medical doctor	People don't work then.
academic advisor	period of time	His/Her parents are dead.
water	person	large; We can buy food and other items there.
holiday	degree	
psychiatrist	store	He/She is trained to talk to students about their academic problems.
bachelor	✓device	
Ph.D.	man	clear; colorless; It consists of two parts hydrogen and one part oxygen (H_2O).
supermarket	child	
		People consult him/her about their emotional problems.
		✓mechanical; time-telling; It is worn on a band about the wrist.
		most advanced; graduate; A university student can receive it.

EXERCISE 7–2

Categorization (Formal Definition)

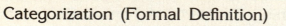

Directions: Following is a chart listing ten terms. Fill in the chart for each of the terms. Then write one-sentence formal definitions for *five* of them.

TERM	GENERAL CLASS	DISTINGUISHING FEATURES
A cafeteria	Restaurant	Self-service
A pencil		
A rose		
The metric system		
A joke		
A canoe		
Zinc		
A loveseat		
A carrot		
A laundromat		

The Extended Definition

When the general class and distinguishing features have been given, the writer may then go on to expand or *extend* a formal definition by giving additional information about the term being defined. This might include such things as a physical description or a list of the advantages of the item. In the case of a wristwatch, for instance, the writer might want to comment on variety in appearance and popularity. Notice that in the following paragraph on the wristwatch, all of this information has been included.

> A wristwatch is a mechanical device which is used for telling time. Its main advantage over other types of time-telling devices (such things as clocks, sundials, or hourglasses) is that it is small enough to be worn on the wrist, so that one can easily know the time by looking down. Wristwatches come in various shapes and sizes, but all have one thing in common: a band or strap with which they may be attached to the wrist. In the United States, where time is money, practically everyone wears a wristwatch.

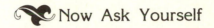Now Ask Yourself

In which sentence of the preceding paragraph do you find evidence of the following:

1. Enumeration? _____

2. Cause-effect? _____

3. Comparison-contrast? _____

4. Examples-details? _____

EXERCISE 7–3

Paragraph Writing: Extended Definition

Phase 1: Exploring Your Topic

Definitions: Referring back to Exercise 7–2, choose *two* of the formal definitions you wrote and develop each of them into a short paragraph of extended definition. In planning your paragraphs, you will want to consider including the following kinds of information using the methods of development and support they call for.

Various kinds or types—Enumeration
Historically interesting information—Chronology
How it works—Process
Advantages or disadvantages—Cause-Effect

Differences from others in the same class—Contrast.
Examples—Supporting Material

If you are working with a partner or in groups, you may wish to show your plan to your classmates to see if the development you have chosen is appropriate.

Phase 2: Writing the First Draft

Directions: Write the first draft of two paragraphs in which you extend your formal definitions. Your paragraphs should give the reader a thorough idea of the meaning of the words you are defining. When you are finished, you may wish to show your work to a classmate to see if your definition is complete.

Phase 3: Making Your Language Accurate

Directions: After you have revised your definitions based on your classmate's suggestions, you will want to check them for correct usage. Proofread your work for all of the common errors we have discussed thus far.

Another common error is the **sentence fragment.** This is a group of words which ends with a period but which is not really a sentence, because it is missing either a *subject* or a *predicate.* Notice the following example of this type of error.

> A wristwatch, which is a mechanical device used for telling
> time and is attached to the wrist.

This group of words is not a sentence, because there is no verb to go with "wristwatch". It is simply a noun followed by a long adjective clause. To correct it, put a comma after "time" and remove the "and", thus making "is attached" the main verb: **A wristwatch, which is a mechanical device used for telling time, is attached to a strap.**

Now look at a second example of this type of error.

> First, has always meant providing your family with a decent
> standard of living with some margin of comfort.

This group of words is not a sentence because the subject is missing. To correct it, add "it" before the verb: **First,** *it* **has always meant providing your family with a decent standard of living with some margin of comfort.**

Proofread your work again to make sure that there are no **sentence fragments.** After you have corrected any errors, recopy this version of your paper and submit it to your teacher.

Problems in Definition

THE CIRCULAR DEFINITION

There are three common problems which may arise in writing definitions. The first problem is that of the *circular definition,* in which the term being defined is repeated in the definition (either the word itself or a word from the same family). For example, if you define *economics* as the study of the economy, you have written a circular definition.

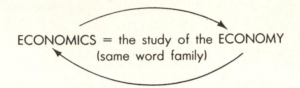

ECONOMICS = the study of the ECONOMY
(same word family)

THE OVEREXTENDED DEFINITION

A second frequent problem is the *overextended definition,* in which the definition can be applied to more things than just the term being defined. If you define *lemonade* as a refreshing drink, for example, you have overextended your definition because there are many other things which fall into this category.

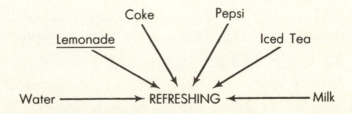

Coke   Pepsi

Lemonade   Iced Tea

Water ⟶ REFRESHING ⟵ Milk

THE OVERRESTRICTED DEFINITION

The third problem area in definition writing is that of *overrestriction.* An overrestricted definition is one in which the term being defined is more comprehensive than the definition (that is, you restrict the item to only a part of its total definition). For example, defining *table* as a place where one eats is overly restrictive, because a table may be used for many other purposes.

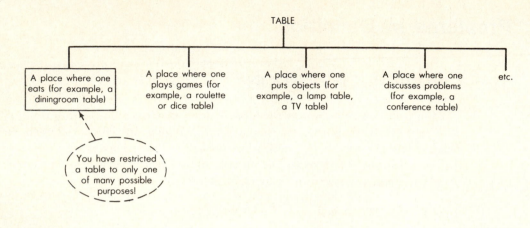

EXERCISE 7–4

Identifying Problems in Definition

Directions: Following are some definitions which do not meet the requirements for a good definition. Explain which problem arises in each. Then rewrite the definition in an acceptable way. Your definitions may be only one or two sentences.

Example

1. A ranch is a place where cowboys live.

   Problem: <u>overrestricted</u>

   Your Definition: <u>A ranch is a large farm, particularly in the American West, on which large herds of cattle, horses, or sheep are raised.</u>

2. Oil is a liquid.

3. Inflation is a process whereby money is inflated.

4. A boot is a rubber covering for the human foot.

5. A university is a place where people study.

6. A grocery store is a place where people buy food.

7. Art is something found in a museum.

8. Pollution is the process whereby chemicals are dumped into rivers.

9. Language is a means of communication.

10. Democracy is a democratic system of government.

The Stipulated Definition

The third type of definition which you may be required to write is one in which you explain how you are using a term *for a particular purpose,* or in which you explain *your particular interpretation of the term.* The word, in the sense in which you understand it, may differ from its usual definition. Like the extended formal definition, the stipulated definition is usually longer than a single sentence.

The kinds of words which require this type of definition are generally abstract ideas or qualities such as *friendship, poverty, justice,* and so on. For instance, you may have to begin a longer composition by defining exactly how you will be using a term in that particular paper:

1. Of all the possible dictionary meanings of the term, you will be using only one, and definitely not the others; or
2. You will be using the term in a very special sense, not to be found in the dictionary (in a personal essay, this may mean making clear your own interpretation of a word; in a philosophy course, it may mean giving a clear explanation of how a particular philosopher uses the term).

EXERCISE 7–5

Analyzing Stipulated Definitions

Directions: Read the following three paragraphs of stipulated definition. Answer the questions which follow each paragraph.

I.   The American concept of success has not changed much over the two centuries of its existence. The average American thinks about personal success in terms quite different from the rest of the world. First, it has always meant providing your family with a decent standard of living with some margin of comfort. Second, it means ending your life in a higher and more prosperous position than you began it. To an American, it is clear that success is the result of hard work, self-reliance, and is "God's reward" for American virtue. The lesson that success lay in your own hands became ingrained because it was within the reach of any free person. Because Americans have consistently been "successful" within this meaning of the term, they have not altered this view substantially.[1]

---

[1] Adapted from J.W. Anderson, "The Idea of Success," *The Washington Post,* July 4, 1976, p. 62.

Now Ask Yourself

1. Why is this interpretation of success a *stipulated* definition rather than a formal definition? _____

   _____

2. What is the topic sentence? _____

   _____

3. What type of development is used to support the topic sentence (enumeration, process, chronological order, cause-effect, comparison, contrast)?

   _____

   _____

4. What do the following pronouns refer back to in the text? (One of them does not specifically refer back to anything.)

   it (line 4) _____

   it (line 6) _____

   it (line 7) _____

   it (line 7) _____

   it (line 10) _____

   this (line 12) _____

   they (line 12) _____

   this (line 13) _____

II.   When European theorists speak of equality, they commonly mean equal status or equal wealth. When Americans use the same term, they usually mean a competition in which everyone gets an equal start. Most of the great social reforms of the 1960s were designed to bring the poor and the blacks "into the running" on something approaching the same footing as the more prosperous and better educated majority. Giving everyone the vote, teaching children to read, and getting them all through high school with a real chance of college beyond all represent the kind of equality that has enormous support in the United States. The basic arrangement of economic life has always provided a balance: enough equality to permit new initiative to flourish wherever it might arise and enough inequality to reward it. Nowhere else have the rewards been so rich and the distribution so wide.[2]

[2]Ibid., p. 73.

🐦 Now Ask Yourself

1. Why is this interpretation of equality a *stipulated* definition rather than a formal one? _____

_____

2. What is the topic sentence? (Look at the paragraph carefully.) _____

_____

_____

3. What type of development is used to support the topic sentence? _____

_____

_____

4. What do the following pronouns refer to?

they (line 1): _____

they (line 3): _____

them (line 8): _____

it (line 13): _____

*III.   It has been said that by understanding what makes a nation laugh, you can define its people. To Americans, laughter is the great leveler, the crystallizer of our iconoclasm. Jack Kennedy's crack about seeing nothing wrong with appointing his brother Robert to the Cabinet "to give him some legal experience as Attorney General before he goes out to practice law" is an example of the acid touch that is common to American humor. The sense of the comic in the United States centers around our own ridiculousness and around the menace suddenly perceived as no longer threatening. As the popular cartoon character Pogo said: "We have met the enemy and he is us." We tend toward a humor that is fast, frank, and irreverent. A black comedian tells his predominantly white audience, "We finally made it. The first Black man was indicted for income tax evasion. We finally made it . . . into nonviolent crime." A more boisterous form of humor is represented by slapstick: a kick in the pants, a pie in the boss's face, the great chase scene where hundreds of people run wildly about, but no one gets caught. Certainly American humor, with its nothing-sacred air and its capacity to hurt and heal, reveals yet another side of the elusive American character.[3]

[3]Adapted from Shelby Coffey III, "Our Savage Wit," *The Washington Post*, July 4, 1976, p. 166–79.

Now Ask Yourself

1. Why is this interpretation of humor a *stipulated* definition?

   _____

   _____

2. Is the first sentence really the topic sentence? Why or why not? _____

   _____

   _____

3. What type of development is used to support the topic sentence? _____

   _____

   _____

   _____

4. What other words in the paragraph are closely related in meaning to the word *humor*? _____

5. What do the following pronouns refer to?

   it (line 1): _____

   its (line 2) _____

   him, (line 5) _____

   it (line 15): _____

   its (line 19) _____

A final note about stipulated definitions is in order. You have no doubt noticed that the stipulated or personal definition lends itself very easily to various kinds of paragraph development (for example, the previous three paragraphs). This is understandable when you consider the nature of this kind of definition. The writer, as we have said, is defining how *he or she* is going to be using the particular term. In terms of types of paragraph development, this may mean, for example, that the writer

1. will be using the term in several different ways (*enumeration* and/or *contrast*).
2. will be using the term in a way which differs significantly from the dictionary definition (*contrast*).
3. will be showing that the explanation of the term has several different parts (*enumeration*).
4. will be showing how the meaning of the term has changed (*chronological order* and/or *contrast*).
5. will be writing of *causes* or of *effects* in the course of the explanation.

EXERCISE 7–6

Review Exercise: Identifying Paragraph Types

Directions: Identify the types of paragraph development used in Unit 1, Exercise 1–5 (pages 12–13) and Exercise 1–7 (pages 18–21).

Unit One, Exercise 1–5

Paragraph 1: _____

Paragraph 2: _____

Paragraph 3: _____

Paragraph 4: _____

Paragraph 5: _____

Paragraph 6: _____

Unit One, Exercise 1–7

Paragraph 1: _____

Paragraph 2: _____

Paragraph 3: _____

Paragraph 4: _____

Paragraph 5: _____

Paragraph 6: _____

Paragraph 7: _____

Paragraph 8: _____

EXERCISE 7–7

Paragraph Writing: Stipulated Definitions

Phase 1: Exploring Your Topic

Directions: Choose one of the following words and consider what that term means to you (general terms) or how you intend to use it in a particular situation (academic terms). Plan a paragraph in which you will stipulate your personal interpretation of the word's meaning. In planning your paragraph, you will have to consider which method of paragraph development best suits your intended meaning of the word.

General Terms

Success
Friendship
Intelligence

Academic Terms

Scientific inquiry
Language learning
Socialism

If you are working with a partner or in groups, you may wish to show your plan to your classmates to see if it indicates the meaning you intended for the term.

Phase 2: Writing the First Draft

Directions: Write the first draft of a paragraph in which you define a term according to your personal interpretation of it. Try to include a specific example to clarify your stipulated meaning. When you have finished, you may wish to show your work to a classmate to see if your definition is clear.

Phase 3: Making Your Language Accurate

Directions: After you have revised your definition based on your classmate's suggestions, you will want to check it for correct usage. Proofread your work for all of the errors we have discussed thus far, including **sentence fragments.** After you have corrected any errors, recopy this version of your paper and submit it to your teacher.

8

FROM PARAGRAPH
TO COMPOSITION

EXPANDING A PARAGRAPH

Thus far, you have been asked to practice certain skills which lead to the production of well-organized paragraphs, the basic units of composition in English. However, it is rare that you will be asked to write just one paragraph in isolation. Ordinarily, any writing task will involve a series of related paragraphs on a given topic—that is, a composition. If you are able to compose a logical, coherent paragraph, it will not be difficult for you to *expand* that paragraph into a longer composition in which you can develop your topic more fully.

How is this done? One possible method has been illustrated for you in the model paragraph and model composition which follow. Study them carefully; then look over the explanatory chart on page 170.

Model Paragraph 1

[1]The Latin influence on American culture, which began with the earliest explorers and continues even today, has been woven into the cultural pattern of America. [2]First, words, such as the place names *Los Angeles* and *Sante Fe* and the commonly-used *adios* (good-bye) and *amigo* (friend), were taken directly from the Spanish language. [3]Latins have also added to the variety of the American diet. [4]Tacos and papayas, for example, are tasty Hispanic additions to the north American table. [5]In addition, the Salsa beat and the rhythms of the tango are musical reminders of the Hispanic presence in the United States. [6]These elements are familiar evidence of the vital Latin contributions to American life.

Model Composition 1

1   We are all aware that American culture is, in fact, a combination of the contributions of all of those who have settled within its borders. From the founding of the country to the present day, immigrants have brought with them the traditions of their native lands, many of which have been interwoven into the cultural patterns of their new homeland. Immigrants from Latin America, who currently comprise about 8 percent of the total population, are no exception to this rule. Hispanic contributions to American culture are reflected in the words we speak, the foods we consume, and the music we enjoy.

2   The Spanish influence on the English language in the U.S. began with the early explorers and continues even today. Spanish place names, from the *Rio Grande* (in Texas) to *San Francisco* (in California), characterize the southwestern part of the country. Los Angeles, Santa Fe, the Colorado River, and the Mojave desert are all part of the heritage of the early Spanish settlers. Other Spanish words, such as *adios, amigo,*

rodeo, and *adobe,* have actually become part of the English language. More recently, a blend of English and Spanish known as *Spanglish,* producing expressions like *ir al movies* (to go to the movies), has developed, particularly in Texas, California, and south Florida, which have a high concentration of Latino residents.

3   From the gourmet-style *churrasco* (marinated tenderloin of beef) to the everyday taco, Latin food has become an integral part of American dining habits. Foods ranging from black beans and rice in a Cuban restaurant to frozen burritos, tropical papayas, and jalapeno peppers on supermarket shelves are evidence of the Latin influence on the American diet. It is not surprising, therefore, that over $1 billion per year was spent on Mexican food in the United States in the late 1980s.

4   American music, too, has become more diverse as a result of the Latino sound. The Salsa beat has had a startling effect on popular music, just as the rhythms of the tango and the cha-cha-cha have become a part of the repertoire of dance bands throughout the country. Instruments, such as the congas and the timbale, also have their origins in Latin countries. Mariachi bands, Brazilian jazz, and the new Miami Sound are further examples of the strong influence of Hispanic musical traditions on American culture.

5   The language, the food, the music—these are but a small part of what Latin Americans have given to North Americans. In the final analysis, the essence of their contributions to American culture is a *sensibilidad* (a unique sense of style), which prompted *Time* magazine to report, "This 'sensibilidad' is changing the way America looks, the way it eats, dresses, drinks, dances, the way it lives."[1]

[1]Nancy R. Gibbs, "Earth and Fire," *Time,* July 11, 1988, p. 68.

Note the various relationships which exist between the paragraph and the composition:

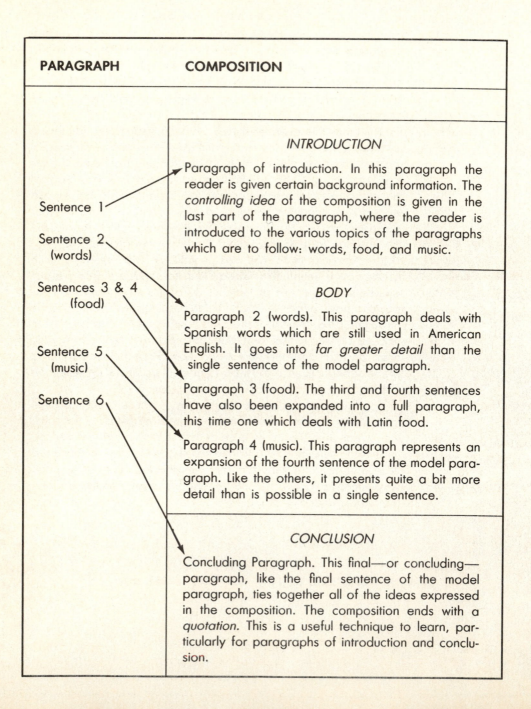

PARAGRAPH	COMPOSITION
	INTRODUCTION
Sentence 1	Paragraph of introduction. In this paragraph the reader is given certain background information. The *controlling idea* of the composition is given in the last part of the paragraph, where the reader is introduced to the various topics of the paragraphs which are to follow: words, food, and music.
Sentence 2 (words)	
	BODY
Sentences 3 & 4 (food)	Paragraph 2 (words). This paragraph deals with Spanish words which are still used in American English. It goes into *far greater detail* than the single sentence of the model paragraph.
Sentence 5 (music)	Paragraph 3 (food). The third and fourth sentences have also been expanded into a full paragraph, this time one which deals with Latin food.
Sentence 6	Paragraph 4 (music). This paragraph represents an expansion of the fourth sentence of the model paragraph. Like the others, it presents quite a bit more detail than is possible in a single sentence.
	CONCLUSION
	Concluding Paragraph. This final—or concluding—paragraph, like the final sentence of the model paragraph, ties together all of the ideas expressed in the composition. The composition ends with a *quotation*. This is a useful technique to learn, particularly for paragraphs of introduction and conclusion.

CONTROLLING IDEA VERSUS TOPIC SENTENCE

You will notice, from reading the preceding model composition, that the first paragraph is unlike any of the paragraphs which you have seen so far in this book. It is called a *paragraph of introduction*. The first thing you will notice about it is that it does not begin with a topic sentence; in fact, there is *no* topic sentence which applies to only that paragraph. Rather, its first sentence introduces the general idea of contributions to American culture. The second sentence restates this idea within a specific period of time. The third sentence, which is even more specific than the second, limits the paragraph to *Hispanic* influences. The fourth and final sentence is the most specific of all: it limits the composition to only *three* Hispanic influences: (1) words, (2) food, and (3) music. We will call this sentence the **controlling idea** of the composition, since it announces in very precise fashion what is to follow. The next three paragraphs then talk about each of these influences. They all have topic sentences; each topic sentence reminds the reader that one specific kind of Hispanic influence is being discussed.

We might say, then, that a controlling idea is *more powerful* and *more general* than a topic sentence. This is not surprising, since a controlling idea controls not a single paragraph, but rather an entire composition. It announces to the reader the main idea of that composition; any topic sentences which follow in subsequent paragraphs help to develop that main idea in much the same way that, in a single paragraph, each sentence helps to develop the idea announced in the topic sentence.

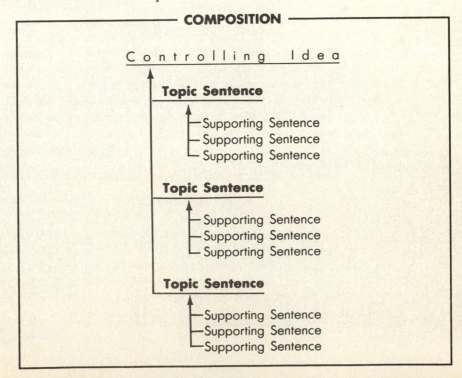

— COMPOSITION —

Controlling Idea

Topic Sentence
— Supporting Sentence
— Supporting Sentence
— Supporting Sentence

Topic Sentence
— Supporting Sentence
— Supporting Sentence
— Supporting Sentence

Topic Sentence
— Supporting Sentence
— Supporting Sentence
— Supporting Sentence

EXERCISE 8–1

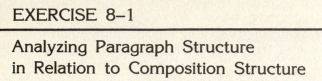

Analyzing Paragraph Structure in Relation to Composition Structure

Directions:

1. Carefully read Model Paragraph 2 and Model Composition 2, which follow.
2. Number each sentence of Model Paragraph 2 and each paragraph of Model Composition 2 in the same way as was done for the first model paragraph and model composition (pages 168–169).
3. Draw arrows to indicate the sentence-paragraph relationships which exist.
4. *Circle the controlling idea* in the model composition.
5. *Underline the topic sentences* of the remaining paragaraphs.
6. *Circle the conclusion.*

Model Paragraph 2

Because Americans are a blend of people from many countries, there are only a few characteristics which can be applied to all Americans. Perhaps the most basic of these is American individuality, which is evident in our history from the days of our founding fathers. The second characteristic shared by all Americans is our paradoxical combination of idealism and practicality. Another typically American feature is the emphasis we place on money and the things it can buy—that is, our materialism. Finally, in practically all American families, our parents exert less influence on us than do parents in other parts of the world. These elements are deeply embedded in the American character, but like many other things American, are subject to change in a relatively short period of time.[2]

Model Composition 2

WE AMERICANS

Since we Americans are a blend of people from many countries, we have a very short history which can properly be called American. Therefore, it is hard to find characteristics which apply to all Americans. We combine many extremes from many different cultures. Nevertheless, we can make some generalizations. Our

[2]Gilbert D. Couts, "We Americans" (unpublished essay, American University, 1977).

main characteristics include individuality, a combination of ideal-ism and practicality, materialism, and a lack of parental influence, all of which permeate our lives.

We Americans value individuality. Our country was founded by strong individuals, and we do not like to be forced into conformity. Therefore, we insist on having a great deal of freedom. Interestingly enough, however, most Americans use this freedom to behave very much like most other Americans, and we are suspicious of those who do not conform. Hippies are individualists, for example, but most Americans do not like them. By the same token, we consider ourselves very faithful to the laws of our country, but there are few among us who would not break one if it was felt that no harm would be done by doing so—such as by exceeding the speed limit or failing to report informally-received cash income on tax forms.

Secondly, we Americans are both practical and idealistic. We place great value on doing things for ourselves, for this is what our pioneer forefathers were forced to do. Many foreign visitors are surprised to find that many couples of comfortable means do their own yardwork, their own housework, their own repairs. On the other hand, we are very idealistic: we think we have the best political, social, and economic system yet devised, and we therefore expect everything to go smoothly. As a result of our idealism, we are easily disillusioned. This is why so many marriages end in divorce—young couples' expectations from marriage are often unrealistically high. Similarly, it helps explain the dissatisfactions and protests of many young people, and even older people, who enjoy one of the highest standards of living in the world.

A third characteristic of us Americans is that money is more important than prestige to us. People work extremely hard, so many, unfortunately, either have little leisure time, or do not know how to enjoy it. Why do we work so hard? It is not to achieve greater status or prestige, but simply to have more of the material objects and comfort that money can buy.

Finally, our parents have less influence on us than parents do in other countries. Many children are left in day-care centers by their working mothers, or with babysitters when their parents go out at night. Furthermore, peer pressure is very great because children's feelings and desires are taken very seriously, and they are given a lot of freedom to form strong personalities. We leave home at a relatively early age, usually after high school, to take jobs and have our own apartments, or to go to college, where we are allowed a great deal of freedom. We choose our own spouses, even if our parents object. And, later in life, when our parents are old and helpless, we often live far away from them; many prefer to put them in nursing homes rather than to have the responsibility of caring for them daily. Many foreigners find this practice heartless. I suppose it is, but like many other qualities we Americans share, it is subject to change over a relatively short period of time.

MIXING METHODS OF PARAGRAPH DEVELOPMENT

You have studied the various methods of arranging supporting sentences (enumeration, process, chronology, cause-effect, and comparison and contrast). You have also seen that examples, details, anecdotes, and facts and statistics can be used with any of these methods.

In like manner, the methods themselves are often *combined* in a longer composition. Good writers will frequently make use of all or a number of these methods to develop their topics. For example, in one paragraph they may enumerate their supporting sentences in descending order; in the next, they may make use of comparison or contrast, quoting statistics to prove their points; another paragraph may use a cause-effect development.

EXERCISE 8–2

Identifying Types of Paragraph Development in a Composition

Directions: Reread Model Composition 2. For each of the paragraphs, identify the type of paragraph development used. If you think that more than one method has been used in the same paragraph, indicate this.

Paragraph 1: <u>cause-effect, enumeration</u>

Paragraph 2: _____

Paragraph 3: _____

Paragraph 4: _____

Paragraph 5: _____

EXERCISE 8–3

Guided Composition Writing:
Information Transfer

Directions: Working alone, in pairs, or in small groups, study the following chart and time line. Then, recopy the composition on a separate sheet of paper, filling in all the blanks. Some blanks will require only one word; others will require more than one. You will have to integrate information from both sources and use words which signal relationships.

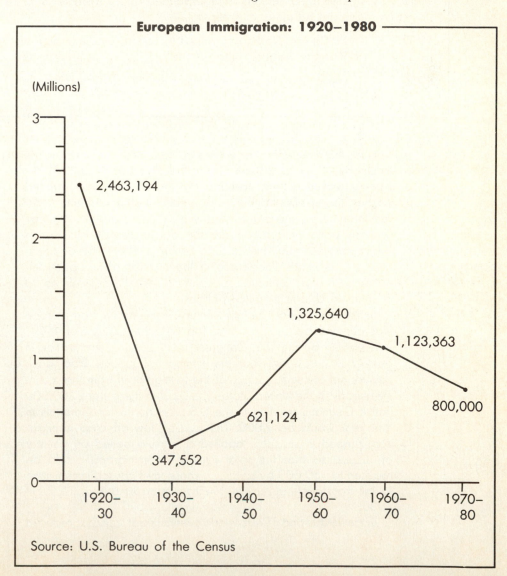

European Immigration: 1920–1980

(Millions)

2,463,194

1,325,640

1,123,363

800,000

621,124

347,552

1920– 30 1930– 40 1940– 50 1950– 60 1960– 70 1970– 80

Source: U.S. Bureau of the Census

Factors Affecting European Immigration to the U.S.

1921	Quota Act: set a quota on the number of immigrants from each country at 3 percent of the number of foreign-born already in the country
1924	National Origins Law: applied a formula to reduce the total number of immigrants to 150,000 by 1927
1930–1940	The Great Depression
1939–1945	The Second World War
1948	Displaced Persons Act: suspended quota restrictions to permit more refugees to enter
1952	McCarran-Walter Act: raised the quota set on immigrants from Western Europe
1956	Immigration Reform Bill: raised the limit on immigrants from the Eastern Hemisphere
---

From the time when the earliest settlers left their native lands in Europe, America (offer) _____ the promise of political, religious, and economic freedom to those who have landed on her shores. During the seventeenth, eighteenth, and nineteenth centuries, the great majority of _____ immigrants came from all parts of Europe, and the dominance of immigration has continued into the _____ century. There have been, _____, dramatic fluctuations in the number of European immigrants in this century _____ world events as well as to changes in U.S. immigration policies.

In the early years of this century, immigration from Europe was affected by _____ laws. The first, the _____ of 1921, was passed by the U.S. Congress (limit) _____ immigration in general. It provided that the number of _____ from each country not exceed _____ of the foreign-born from that country already in the United States. _____, if there were 300,000 native Germans residing in the U.S., the quota for Germans in that year would be 9,000. The _____ law affecting immigration, passed in _____, applied a formula based on country of _____ so that the total number of immigrants would be reduced to 150,000 by _____. These laws caused immigration to fall from over _____ in 1920 to approximately _____ in 1930.

In the 1930s and 1940s, world events (lead) _____ reduced

immigration to the U.S. from Europe. The _____ made it less desirable because the chances for immigrants to improve their economic condition were significantly lessened. _____, potential immigrants (affect) _____ by the Depression and could not afford (move) _____ their families. After the outbreak of _____ in 1939, immigration slowed to an all-time low.

During the postwar years, ____ to ____, there was an influx in the number of immigrants from Europe, (result) _____ a liberalization of the U.S. immigration policy. The _____ of 1948 suspended all quota restrictions to permit refugees from war-torn Europe to enter the country. In _____, the McCarran-Walter Act once again set quotas but established a _____ quota for immigrants from Western Europe. Because of this policy, immigration once again rose to over _____ by the late 1950s.

During the latter part of the twentieth century, other laws (pass) _____ to provide for more equitable immigration opportunities for non-Europeans. _____, there continues to be a steady flow from _____ same countries in Europe which peopled this nation when it was a wilderness. It is probably safe to say that these _____ will continue to come for the same reasons their forebearers did—(live) _____ in a land where they are guaranteed religious, political, and economic freedom.

❧ Now Ask Yourself

1. What development does the controlling idea suggest?
2. How is the information organized into paragraphs?
3. What kind of information is found in the introduction? In the conclusion?

❧ EXERCISE 8–4

Composition Writing: Mixed Methods

Phase 1: Exploring Your Topic

Directions: Expand one of the paragraphs you wrote previously into the first draft of a full composition. Choose from the following:

Unit 3, Exercise 3–9: Enumeration
Unit 4, Exercises 4–6 and 4–11: Process and Chronology

Unit 5, Exercises 5–4 and 5–7: Cause-Effect
Unit 6, Exercises 6–4 and 6–11: Comparison-Contrast

As you are planning your paper, notice that even though your original paragraph may have been one of cause-effect, when it is expanded you will have to make use of other methods of development as well. For instance, the information within each paragraph will probably be **enumerated,** and you may develop a **contrast** within a paragraph to illustrate your point. In other words, when you are writing longer papers, you will find it necessary to make use of several types of paragraph development in order to convey information thoroughly.

Prepare a plan for your paper using the following guidelines:

Introduction

Your original topic sentence will become the controlling idea for your composition and will appear at the *end* of your introductory paragraph. This paragraph should begin with a very general statement about your topic. It should have two or three more sentences which narrow the topic to the specific points you intend to discuss. In other words, your paragraph of introduction should move from general information about your topic to the specific aspects you will write about in this composition. Study the paragraphs of introduction in the two model compositions in this unit and in Exercise 8–3 to get ideas for how to focus attention on a topic and lead up to a controlling idea.

Body

You will want to devote one entire paragraph to each of the points you mentioned in your original paragraph. You will, of course, have to go into greater detail and provide more **examples** for each point than you did in your original paragraph. Remember to begin each paragraph of the body with a topic sentence that tells the reader which point you will be discussing.

Conclusion

You will have to add a paragraph of conclusion. In it, you should summarize, restate, or reemphasize the main ideas in your composition. Notice how the authors of both model compositions in this unit have used a single pronoun—*these*—to remind the reader of all the paragraphs in the body of the composition. You might want to try this technique. You might also want to use an appropriate quotation to conclude your paper.

Phase 2: Writing the First Draft

Directions: Write the first draft of your paper. If you are working in pairs or in groups, show your draft to your classmates to see if you have added enough information to fully develop the points you have mentioned in your controlling idea. Revise this draft based on your classmates' suggestions.

Phase 3: Making Your Language Accurate

Directions: After you have revised your work based on your classmates' suggestions, you will want to check it for usage. Proofread your paper for all of the common errors we have discussed thus far. In addition, make sure that all of the words are spelled correctly. When you have corrected any errors, recopy this version and submit it to your teacher.

EXERCISE 8–5

Composition Writing: Mixed Methods

Phase 1: Exploring Your Topic

Directions: Prepare a plan for a full composition based on one of the following topics. First, make a list of all the influences or characteristics (depending on which topic you choose) that you can think of. Then limit your discussion to the three which you feel are most significant. Plan an introduction which begins with general statements about your topic and ends with a specific statement of your controlling idea. Think of ways you might stress your controlling idea in your conclusion. You may wish to refer back to the model compositions in this unit for ideas. If you are working with a partner or in groups, you may wish to show your plan to your classmates to see if it is appropriate for the topic chosen.

General Topic

the characteristics you feel are shared by the people in your society

Essay Questions

Discuss the influences of another culture on the culture of (your society).

Phase 2: Writing the First Draft

Directions: Write the first draft of an essay in which you develop the points in your controlling idea. Your paper should have an introduction, three body paragraphs, and a conclusion. You may use any method of paragraph development which suits the topic. Be sure to use concrete examples to make your general statements clear. When you are finished, you may wish to show your work to your classmates to see if you have been successful in developing your ideas.

Phase 3: Making Your Language Accurate

Directions: After you have revised your work based on your classmates' suggestions, you will want to check it for correct usage. Proofread your paper for all of the common errors we have discussed thus far and for spelling. When you have corrected any errors, recopy this version and submit it to your teacher.

INDEX